Management for P

The Springer series *Management for Professionals* comprises high-level business and management books for executives. The authors are experienced business professionals and renowned professors who combine scientific background, best practice, and entrepreneurial vision to provide powerful insights into how to achieve business excellence.

Lars Michael Bollweg

Data Governance for Managers

The Driver of Value Stream Optimization and a Pacemaker for Digital Transformation

 Springer

Lars Michael Bollweg
Dortmund, Germany

ISSN 2192-8096   ISSN 2192-810X   (electronic)
Management for Professionals
ISBN 978-3-662-65173-5   ISBN 978-3-662-65171-1   (eBook)
https://doi.org/10.1007/978-3-662-65171-1

In Cooperation with Davide Iannella and Angelika Schneider

Foreword

Data and its proper use and application are finally receiving the attention they deserve in German business. The legal requirements that have arisen as a result of the introduction of the European General Data Protection Regulation (GDPR) are making a significant contribution to this change. For the first time, there was a notable risk for companies in the incorrect use of data. However, that protection against risks should not be the only reason to have the own data under control is shown to us by the economic giants from Silicon Valley. They are dominating the stock markets for several years with data-driven business models. Accordingly, the motto of the hour is: If you want to develop your business, you have to understand your data and use it profitably. Process improvement and automation, new business areas and intelligent, fact-based decisions, everything stands and falls with data, the knowledge of data, and the skills required to use this data correctly. Data Governance forms the basis for organizations to face this challenging task.

The establishment of a data organization capable of acting on data issues is therefore at the heart of a Data Governance implementation program. However, if a Data Governance program is to have a chance of success, it must focus on soft as well as on hard factors. For example, it is essential that a cultural change toward a data-centric company is accompanied and promoted by Data Governance. Data must therefore not only be referred to as an asset, but also be treated as such. This is important and old paradigms must be questioned for this purpose, particularly when dealing with an economic asset that can be replicated almost free of charge and being sold without losing it. This complexity coupled with the need to change the way companies work and the need to learn new skills across the enterprise, highlights the challenging scope of implementing Data Governance.

As head of the program to implement Data Governance at Westnetz GmbH, it is Dr. Lars Bollweg's job to bundle this multitude of perspectives into a joint initiative. In addition to stringent support from top management, it is thanks to his energy and ingenuity that Data Management at Westnetz is now more than a task for a few, but an essential part of the entire company. Once again, Data Governance is not a topic for the ivory tower. Data Governance lives in the decentralized units that work with the data every day and that are responsible for its quality and proper provision. Above all, Data Governance only really comes to life when no member of a Data Management unit is required to use or understand data professionally.

The steps and principles described in this book for implementing Data Governance in an organization are not pure theory, but come from the lived practice of a successful program. Both the roles described and the given approach therefore exist outside a laboratory situation in a living and breathing company. At Westnetz, too, the road to the first successes of Data Governance was long, and it is still way to go. However, take the advices given in this book to heart and persevere. Only stamina and full conviction in the matter will lead to success. The good thing is—the work is worth it!

Data Management, Westnetz GmbH   Henning Krings
Dortmund, Germany

Contents

About the Author

Lars Michael Bollweg As Head of IT-Service Strategy, Dr. Lars Michael Bollweg is responsible for IT Governance in a large German energy company. As former Data Officer and Head of Data Governance he was also responsible for the implementation of the Data Governance program. Prior to his time in the energy industry, he was employed as a consultant for digitalization and strategy at one of the largest food retail groups in Europe. He holds a Ph.D. in business informatics on the digital transformation of retail companies. He is also the author of a number of scientific publications on the research topic "digital transformation" and a lecturer for Big Data, Data Science and programming languages at private and public universities.

Supported by

• Angelika Schneider—Deputy Head of the Department of Business and Housing Management

• Davide Iannella—Student of Business Informatics and Student Assistant in a large German energy company

Introduction

1

Abstract

This book is not a book about data. This statement may surprise you and perhaps more completely correct is the statement: This book is not a book "just" about data. That is because this book is a book about data, business processes, and IT systems. It is a book that tells you how companies can generate and realize valuable impulses for the further development of data, corporate processes, IT systems, and the entire digital transformation with the help of professional Data Management and the establishment of a responsive data organization (Data Governance).

But let's start from the beginning:

Every day, an organization creates, uses, maintains, and, deletes thousands and thousands of pieces of data, and with each additional day, it becomes more (see Fig. 1.1).

And even though data often lies invisible, deeply hidden behind the graphical user interfaces of systems in databases, the professional management of this data today is one of the most crucial factors for sustainable business success tomorrow. This is especially true for industries in which physical process chains have already reached a high level of optimization and productivity. In these companies, the potential that can be leveraged through managed data and information flows, e.g., through automation or decision support, is the next logical step to further increasing productivity and the key to digital transformation.

But it is precisely the management of digital transformation and thus the management of this ongoing change process fueled by digital technologies that is still a major, often unresolved challenge for many traditional companies and organizations. Yet, there is usually no lack of good ideas and the right approaches. Companies fail to develop modern and innovative solutions more often because of their own

© Springer-Verlag GmbH Germany, part of Springer Nature 2022
L. M. Bollweg, *Data Governance for Managers*, Management for Professionals,
https://doi.org/10.1007/978-3-662-65171-1_1

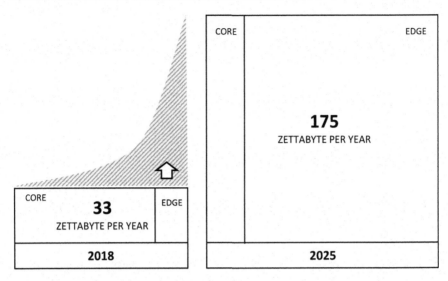

Fig. 1.1 EU forecast of data generation in 2025 (EU 2019) © Lars Michael Bollweg 2022. All Rights Reserved

existing, often outdated IT and management structures, than because of a lack of potential areas for development.

Rigid IT systems, sluggish process development, and constant silo thinking are just a few prominent examples of a multitude of historically grown undesirable developments that are often found within companies and organizations. The fact that these well-known problems are still holding back a large number of companies in their digital development today shows very impressively that organizational responsiveness, i.e., the ability to respond to the constantly changing digital challenges in the context of digital transformation with the further development of data, processes, and systems, has not yet reached the necessary level of maturity across the board. And because digital transformation is primarily perceived within and outside of organizations as a technical development, companies often lack a focus on the further development and empowerment of precisely these existing management structures in order to achieve a higher level of maturity.

And this is where well-planned Data Governance comes in. Data Governance is, of course, on the one hand the professionalization of the handling of data in the company, but Data Governance is also a change management process accompanying the digital transformation with a direct influence on the continuous organizational development around data, processes, and IT systems.

In this sense, the introduction of professional Data Management with the help of Data Governance is a dual driver of digital transformation—both technologically and organizationally.

Accordingly, the added value of Data Governance does not lie solely in the professional management of data and the establishment of a data organization (e.g., merely in data quality management or the assignment of data responsibilities).

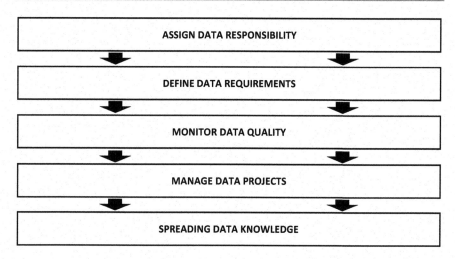

Fig. 1.2 Fundamentals of Data Governance © Lars Michael Bollweg 2022. All Rights Reserved

The real added value of Data Governance arises and unfolds precisely from these points: By empowering the data organization, Data Governance makes a particularly decisive contribution to business transformation. This is because the data organization provides impetus for data, process, and system optimization and thus forms the basis for the development of a data-driven corporate culture.

The foundations for this dual role of Data Governance are created by the key practices of Data Management and the resulting data organization: (1) assign data responsibilities, (2) define data requirements, (3) improve and monitor data quality, (4) manage data projects, and (5) disseminate data knowledge (see Fig. 1.2).

Building on professional Data Management and a responsive data organization, the power of Data Governance to drive the digital transformation of a company always emerges when professional Data Management works together with professional process and system management and all units jointly initiate and implement holistic developments.

An exemplary tool for this is the method of data-driven value stream optimization. By taking a joint look at data, processes, and systems, this method identifies existing potential for optimization and further development (see Fig. 1.3). In the fourth part of the book, the method of data-driven value stream optimization is comprehensively explained and introduced.

Hopefully, it has already become clear by this point that the approach to implementing and establishing Data Governance presented in this book is more than "just" data. And that Data Governance is more than just Data Management. Data Governance, in the reading of this book, is a logical and natural part of organizational development. Data Governance, in this reading, sees itself as the foundation, the bedrock of digital transformation, and as a service provider for the processes and IT systems and an enabler for the innovation and development projects of all other organizational areas.

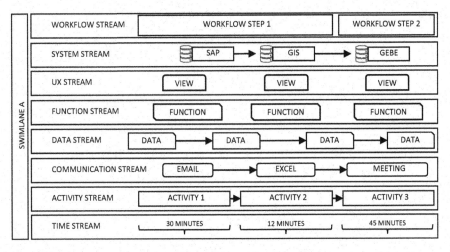

Fig. 1.3 Dimensions of data-driven value stream optimization © Lars Michael Bollweg 2022. All Rights Reserved

1	**BASICS OF DATA GOVERNANCE** BASICS
2	**PLANNING DATA GOVERNANCE** DESIGN
3	**IMPLEMENTATION OF DATA GOVERNANCE** IMPLEMENT
4	**REGULAR OPERATION OF A DATA GOVERNANCE** RUN
5	**MEASURING THE SUCCESS OF DATA GOVERNANCE** CONTROL

Fig. 1.4 Overview of structure and contents © Lars Michael Bollweg 2022. All Rights Reserved

The target audience for this book is managers and executives who are about to or in the middle of planning, implementing, and adding value to Data Governance (from responsive data organizations to successful data projects) in everyday business. In particular, the motivation for writing this book is to also help you and your company master and solve the digital transformation and the many digital challenges that come with it by implementing Data Governance. In order to implement this intention in a targeted manner, the contents of this book have been structured into five parts and eleven chapters (see Fig. 1.4).

In the first part, **"Basics,"** the fundamentals of Data Governance are taught and essential terms and structures are introduced to create a common understanding for the subsequent chapters and to enable the successful implementation of Data Governance.

The second part, **"Design,"** is about the basic planning and design of a Data Governance program and how to make your planning a success.

The third part, **"Implement,"** discusses the adoption and implementation of Data Governance and provides guidance on how you can overcome the biggest hurdles in the change process.

In the fourth part **"Run,"** it is shown how a company can not only professionally manage data with the support of a responsive Data Governance, but also use it for data-driven data, process, and system development and as a driver for digital transformation. The chapter concludes with an outlook on the required connection points of Data Governance to the digital production line so that the identified potential developments can also be put into practice.

The last part, **"Control,"** deals with the introduction of a maturity scale for measuring the success of the implementation activities related to Data Governance. In the final part of the book, all relevant decision points for the planning, implementation, and regular operation of Data Governance are listed in a list of principles.

Our goal is that when you have read this book, you will be able to answer a large number of your existing questions about Data Governance:

- What is Data Governance?
- What are the roles and structures of Data Governance?
- How is data responsibility or data ownership assigned?
- What skills does a Data Management department or team need to run successful Data Governance?
- What do you need to think about when successfully developing an implementation strategy for Data Governance?
- How can you use data projects to generate immediate added value for the company and thus a high level of acceptance for the implementation of Data Governance?
- How can you optimize, harmonize, and End2End manage data, processes, and systems via the value contributions of Data Governance, and what methods can help you do this?
- How can you sustainably change the corporate culture with Data Governance and benefit from this change in the long term?

For orientation and as a learning aid, we summarize all the important decision-making points of each chapter in simple principles. Use these 30 principles, which you will also find listed in Chap. 8, as a source of inspiration and later as a shortcut if you only want to review individual sections of this book.

For better readability, the masculine form is used in this book when referring to persons and personal nouns. Corresponding terms apply in principle to all genders in the interests of equal treatment. The abbreviated form of language is for editorial reasons only and does not imply any valuation. Quite the contrary is the case. All the roles, process models, and methods mentioned here in the book benefit from a diverse group of employees and users, since innovation and development thrive on different life experiences, changes of perspective, and different points of view.

And before you are now released on your journey through this book and into the topic of Data Governance, one more personal recommendation:

If you set yourself or the organization in which you work on the path to becoming a data-centric company, a data-centric organization, then you are on the right path. However, do not forget: data is also only a means to an end, and in most cases, the end is called "business success." True to the motto:

Data doesn't matter.
It's what you derive from it.
It's what you do with it that matters.
(Data Management Idiom—Unknown Author)

In an ever faster changing digital world, keep in mind the direct added values for your tasks, your projects and of course your company at every development step. Yes, create strategic foundations within long-term development projects such as Data Governance, but at the same time serve, even in small steps, the short-term, existing requirements of the organization. Keep an eye on the big challenges and move the big tanker in the right direction, but look as directly as possible for contributions and value-added projects for the day-to-day business. Implement this "operational philosophy of direct value-adds" into your implementation and transformation plans, as well as to the building blocks of your Data Governance program, from the start, and you will successfully transform your organization. From the ground up and for the better.

Reference

European Union (EU) (2019) European data strategy. https://ec.europa.eu/info/strategy/priorities-2019-2024/europe-fit-digital-age/european-data-strategy_de#daten-governance

Part I

Basics

What Is Data Governance?

2

Abstract

If you ask ten data managers what Data Governance actually is or how you define Data Governance, you will usually get ten different answers. This is because every Data Governance implementation, like every company, is unique. This makes it all the more important to create a common basis at the beginning, from which you can then derive the right decisions and course settings for customized Data Governance in your company at a later stage. To this end, we start with a simple definition and then, as the complexity increases, we introduce all aspects and fields of action of Data Governance step by step in an understandable and practical manner. Experience has shown that many people find the topic of Data Governance very abstract and difficult to grasp at first. The aim of this chapter is to help you to transform this abstract vagueness of Data Governance as a concept into your own clear understanding of the practical processes and activities behind the term Data Governance.

2.1 Basics and Definition of Data Governance

As a starting point and to establish a basic understanding, we will be guided by the following definition for Data Governance in the first chapters:

▶ *Data Governance is the structured integration of Data Management practices (procedures and methods) in the organizational structures and processes of a company.*

The charming thing about this definition is that it is very short. And of course that is also the problem with this definition; it is too short. Of course, a bit more context is needed to understand Data Governance comprehensively. To achieve a real

L. M. Bollweg, *Data Governance for Managers*, Management for Professionals,
https://doi.org/10.1007/978-3-662-65171-1_2

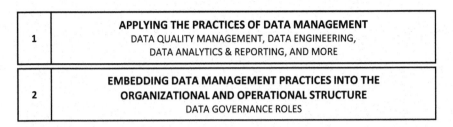

Fig. 2.1 Basic components and goals of Data Governance © Lars Michael Bollweg 2022. All Rights Reserved

understanding, it therefore makes sense to go through the two most important points of the definition in detail (see Fig. 2.1):

(1) **Application of Data Management Practices:**
    Data Management is not a young discipline. For more than 30 years, practitioners and researchers have been developing "best practices" for handling data in companies and organizations (DAMA International 2017). Key practices will be discussed in more depth throughout this book. But in broad terms, we are talking about topics such as data quality management, data engineering, data analytics and reporting, and many more. Since time immemorial, these practices have been taught in professional, technical, and higher education institutions, in further education institutes, and now often in online courses. In addition, one can find a variety of publications on this complex of topics, e.g., in textbooks and research articles. The practices of Data Management are the essence of these years of experience of the field of "Data Management," and they describe nothing else than the professional handling of data in companies. But even though Data Management as a field builds on such a long history and such a large body of knowledge, applications and implementations of these practices into enterprise operations are still at a very low level of maturity in most companies.
    Data Governance is therefore a tool to bring these practices (procedures and methods) to bear in the company.

(2) **Structured integration into the process organization:**
    Even though there are always isolated experts in the handling of data in companies, the application of Data Management practices is still not anchored in the breadth of the organization in accordance with the importance and significance for the success of the company (buzzwords: digitalization/digital transformation) (Seiner 2014). And what is unfortunate, mostly, they are not applied at all.
    Dealing with data and Data Management in general is still far too often treated as a "sideline" activity that requires neither guidance nor specifications within the company.
    Data Governance is therefore also a tool for anchoring the application of Data Management practices in breadth, i.e., in all departments, and in depth among all

THE THREE LEVELS OF A

DATA GOVERNANCE

3	**DATA PROJECTS** FURTHER DEVELOPMENT OF DATA TO SOLVE PAIN POINTS AND RAISE DEVELOPMENT POTENTIALS
2	**APPLYING THE PRACTICES OF DATA MANAGEMENT** DATA QUALITY MANAGEMENT, DATA ENGINEERING, DATA ANALYTICS & REPORTING, AND MORE
1	**DATA ORGANIZATION** IMPLEMENTATION OF THE DATA GOVERNANCE ROLES IN THE ORGANIZATIONAL AND OPERATIONAL STRUCTURE

Fig. 2.2 The three levels of a Data Governance © Lars Michael Bollweg 2022. All Rights Reserved

employees of the company organization. By creating Data Governance roles, which are given responsibilities and tasks, Data Governance as a whole has a positive impact on the development of the organizational structure. From the organizational structure, the Data Governance roles then have a positive effect on the development of the process organization, as the roles are empowered with procedures and methods via Data Management practices to meet the upcoming data challenges. Each Data Governance role has clearly defined tasks that must be solved according to clearly defined specifications and procedures within defined degrees of freedom.

Sometimes a picture helps to make Data Governance even more tangible: In very simple terms, Data Governance creates an organizational chart around data in which you can see, for example, who or which role is responsible for which data assets in the company, who has been tasked with maintaining data, who has the greatest knowledge about defined parts of the data, and who is to be involved in changes and further developments of data and data processes.

To further solidify our understanding of Data Governance, let's change perspective once again and deepen our view a bit (see Fig. 2.2):

At the lowest and most fundamental level, the basis of Data Governance is the data organization (the organizational chart around data). This also means that developing the data organization and defining the roles within Data Governance is one of the most important and challenging activities in implementing Data Governance.

Building on the data organization, Data Governance encounters the real data only at the second level. The data organization creates the framework for the professional handling of data and for the application of Data Management practices. This includes documenting the data, assigning data responsibility (data ownership) within the organization, and from there, developing the data on the third level. Data Governance is not an end in itself, and today it is no longer sufficient for Data Governance to focus purely on controlling data. A successful Data Governance implementation focuses on the further development of the data from the very beginning. This usually takes place in so-called data projects. Enabling the company to implement this form of further development projects in a targeted and efficient manner is the real driving force behind Data Governance. Accordingly, a Data Governance that is able to implement digital developments in a targeted manner is an ideal driver for the overall digital transformation of a company.

The background and interaction of the three levels of Data Governance presented and the importance of adhering to the sequence during implementation will be explained in more detail in the following chapters. Now, at the beginning, it is important to understand that the goal of any successful Data Governance is to support a company in taking on the challenges of digital transformation and mastering them successfully with the help of a functioning data organization.

> **Principle 1:** Data Governance anchors Data Management in the organizational and operational structure of a company. Data Governance ensures that data accountabilities, coordination and optimization processes, as well as procedural models and standards are practiced uniformly and transparently throughout the company.

As mentioned earlier, Data Governance is not an end in itself. It is therefore important to communicate the advantages or value contributions of Data Governance in the company right from the start. The potential value contributions that can be leveraged by Data Governance can be categorized into five core areas (see Fig. 2.3):

(1) **Operational excellence:** Data Governance contributes to optimizing data-driven operational processes.
(2) **Analytics, reporting, and decision support:** Data Governance supports the management and decision-making level with optimized data layers and analyses, reporting and data-based decision-making aids for strategic and operational decisions.
(3) **Compliance and risk management:** Data Governance supports the company in complying with corporate regulations and in implementing statutory requirements. In this way, Data Governance helps companies to successfully manage data-based risks.
(4) **Collaboration and data literacy:** Data Governance deepens collaboration between business units and IT and acts as a multiplier for data literacy in the company.
(5) **Digital transformation and automation:** Data Governance lays the foundations for digital transformation and drives the use of automation and

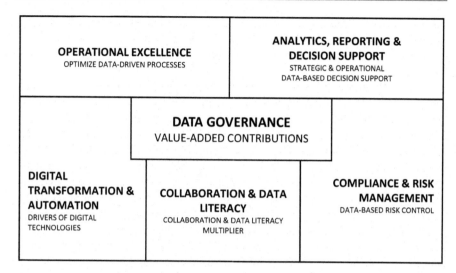

Fig. 2.3 Value contributions of Data Governance © Lars Michael Bollweg 2022. All Rights Reserved

decision support systems (e.g., with artificial intelligence) within corporate processes and systems.

2.2   Levels of Complexity

Now that an initial sense of what Data Governance actually is has been established, let's start at the very beginning and ask ourselves the crucial question: Why is Data Governance such a big challenge for many companies in the first place? The answer is simple, but requires some explanation. The great difficulty for companies lies in managing the high complexity of the often very abstract topic of "data."

Let's simplify a bit and imagine the complexity of data challenges for companies stacked on five different levels. Each individual level alone is a major challenge, but with each additional level that must be managed simultaneously by the company, the complexity increases many times over directly (see Fig. 2.5).

(1) Requirement-Based Description of Reality

On the lowest of the five levels, we encounter the first dimension of the complex challenges in dealing with data: the description of reality according to requirements. What sounds philosophical is the most fundamental and important dimension in dealing with data: the content and the expression of the data. Data always describes a reality. This reality can be physical, e.g., a number of transport boxes, or virtual, e.g., values of bitcoins. However, the state that the reality describes is not crucial at this moment. It is only important to understand that no matter how good a description of reality is, the description can only ever encompass a subset of reality. To generate data, we compress, reduce, and prioritize reality. We explicitly do not capture parts of reality because they do not seem important enough to us. In other words, we inevitably and deliberately omit parts of reality (DAMA International 2017; Soares 2015a).

This compression process in data creation should be based on conscious decisions. And these conscious decisions should be based on existing requirements in the company. If this is not the case, we are talking about poor data quality. Good data quality meets the requirements ("fit to use"), ideally the current ones and in the medium term the future ones. Poor data quality means that the data does not fit the company's requirements ("unfit to use"). If the data quality is poor, it must be reworked or the data must even be created from scratch. It becomes clear that it is precisely in the data creation process that the critical course is set for the success of a company. Does a company work economically with data or does it have high preparation costs? This decision is often made at the very beginning of a data lifecycle and determines how structured and reflective a company is in dealing with the data request process in order to arrive at an optimal description of reality through data that meets the requirements.

(2) Complex IT Landscapes and Interoperability
If we look at the next level up, we encounter the next incremental form in the complexity of data challenges: IT systems. The realities described in data are stored within databases. These databases typically reside within system architectures and come into play within system functionalities of applications as well as between IT systems via their interfaces. These systems with the data in turn reside on an IT infrastructure, such as servers or computers. Data therefore lies at the center of a network of systems/applications (software) and IT infrastructure (hardware). Together, they serve to fulfill the company's processes.

Unfortunately for a company, the level of IT systems is not mastered with the adaptation of data to the creation system (source system). A single company has to solve a multitude of tasks within interrelated process chains, and no matter how hard they try, to date no company has succeeded in mapping all corporate processes within just one software on just one server. Companies therefore almost inevitably use a variety of different hardware and software solutions to achieve their business goals. And it is therefore in the nature of individually assembled and grown IT landscapes that data of a company within a source system must be adapted to the requirements of a multitude of other systems right away, so that "interoperability" is achieved (see Fig. 2.4).

Interoperability is the seamless interaction of different hardware and software components within an IT architecture. The highest possible level of interoperability is therefore also the goal for a company and its IT landscape, so that information and data can be exchanged smoothly between systems. You can think of it like a production line. All the machines have to work together in perfect time along the assembly line to ensure that production runs as smoothly as possible. And it is precisely here that the second level of complexity in dealing with data unfolds its unpleasant depth. Because as soon as data leaves its creation system, in-depth

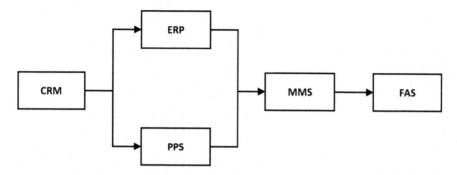

Fig. 2.4 Simplified representation of IT system landscape (Interoperability). (The abbreviations used in this figure stand for widely used enterprise applications. *CRM* Customer Relationship Management System, *ERP* Enterprise Resource Planning, *PPS* Production Planning System, *MMS* Merchandise Management System, *FAS* Financial Accounting System) © Lars Michael Bollweg 2022. All Rights Reserved

knowledge of the reality described and at the same time of the requirements of the data along the downstream systems is necessary in order to achieve interoperability that meets the requirements. Ideally, to manage this complexity, a company creates a complete and transparent overview of how systems and data interfaces interact. Extending this representation to provide an overview of the possible data keys is usually helpful in facilitating the necessary further development of the systems and interfaces. But such a system and process data model is costly and only pays off in companies that are actively working on the further development of their infrastructure. In addition to the creation effort, there is a permanent maintenance effort, which is central and difficult to manage for companies without Data Governance. Without an overview of the information and data flows, the system interfaces, and the potential for linkages, e.g., for automation, this level can hardly be mastered.

(3) Data Maintenance by Employees
Fittingly, the third level of complexity in handling data arises along the maintenance of the data. After all, handling data is not a purely technical task that can be outsourced to IT departments. In the end, all systems and databases are used and controlled by people, who are to be found in large numbers in the business departments. Therefore, it is not surprising that the business departments of a company are truly the biggest data producers. And despite the fact that the departments generate the data, it is often difficult for these departments in traditional companies to accept the professional handling of data as an original and separate task. This is why it is so difficult for companies on a day-to-day basis to trace the origin of inadequate data generation and to safeguard data quality for the future by taking appropriate measures (e.g., input validation). It often takes a great deal of effort for companies to get all the necessary players around the same table for decision-making in the event of data changes or further developments. As a result, such companies have problems driving forward the digital transformation, even

though this is actually the key to further productivity gains along the company's processes. Organizing and empowering employees to handle data professionally is therefore naturally also an important building block for future corporate success.

(4) Business Processes and Legal Requirements

On the next level of complexity in dealing with data, we encounter corporate processes and legal requirements. These two terms represent the currently most effective drivers, internal and external, for the professional handling of data (Data Governance) and generate further complexity to be managed. Business processes as internal drivers serve to fulfill business objectives. They are the very essence of a company and the benchmark for all actions. Few companies can or want to allow themselves an agenda apart from corporate processes and therefore streamline their organization and operations to make the cycle times for processes as short or as efficient as possible. Traditionally, this optimization has been heavily focused on the physical process steps and has provided very large productivity gains for companies in this area over the past few decades. The entire "Lean Development" is based on this paradigm. Today, however, the majority of physical process chains are at a high level of optimization, so automation through digitalization is the next important step toward increasing productivity. However, automation requires a particularly high level of data quality and interoperability. Unfortunately, this paradigm shift has not yet arrived at many companies, which is why even today only a few companies consider the potential of professional Data Management for their corporate success in their strategy.

This "strategic blind spot" in corporate development leads to uncontrolled and uncoordinated measures and decisions in companies in the face of new legal requirements, e.g., the introduction of the General Data Protection Regulation (GDPR) and its strict specifications and threats of punishment. These "panic-stricken" companies, out of blind obedience to meeting legal requirements, like to develop isolated parallel organizations, which are completely limited to just meeting these legal requirements. In doing so, companies often forget to utilize these externally enforced development impulses in the sense of the internal further development of the company. A classic example of this are GDPR organizations such as data protection or deletion coordination. These organizations work their way through the data structures of a company to identify personal data and ensure its deletion within the framework of the legal requirements, unfortunately, all too often without recognizing the synergies to manage and evolve data, data processes, and system infrastructures. Thus, one unit does exactly the right thing and deals intensively with the data in the company, but only for the legislator and forgets about the company itself. It is neglected to simultaneously look for potentials for the company and to make them visible. In this way, a company gets lost in the complexity of the many parallel organizations and processes when meeting external requirements, instead of building a functioning data organization that can serve the legal and corporate requirements.

(5) Volume, Variety, Velocity, and Veracity

Finally, we turn to the last level of complexity: the volume, variety, velocity, and veracity of data. These four points are also known as the "Big Four V's of Big Data." They describe the diversity of the challenge in dealing with big data in enterprises. The sheer number of data (volume) is often the first and most obvious challenge facing enterprises. Surprisingly, however, this is the easiest to solve today. Distributed systems (e.g., Hadoop clusters with MapReduce) today make it possible to handle this high throughput of data smoothly by processing data in parallel. It becomes more challenging when the data is generated at a very high speed (velocity) (e.g., meter values of a measuring point) and then has to be processed in real time. However, modern systems are able to cope with this when the data is as standardized as possible. But it gets complicated when we imagine the same with unstandardized, often unstructured data (variety), which must not only simply be passed through a channel, but must also be processed and evaluated in the same breath. And the peak of stress is reached when this colorful bouquet of data is then also full of data quality problems and requires ongoing validation (veracity).

So it's about more than the sheer volume of data; it's about the variety of different data and the high speed at which it is created and of course how it moves through the systems. And this is not the end of the story either. Because in the end, every employee in the company also creates, uses, maintains, and deletes data, further adding to the complexity. And the sheer amount of existing data within companies continues to grow exponentially. A rule of thumb says that 90% of the data in the world today, and thus also of the data in companies, is less than 3 years old.

This means that in the next three years we will produce 9 times more data than we already have in our systems today. Of course, this rule does not claim to be correct, but it does vividly illustrate why it is no longer sufficient to prepare for tomorrow's digital transformation with yesterday's organizational structures. The digital transformation is already underway today, and it is only now really picking up speed.

Companies that are already substantially challenged with the management of their data to their performance and capacity limits will run into critical situations in the next few years. It is already foreseeable that the major development barrier will not be the lack of employee expertise in topics such as "artificial intelligence"; it will be the lack of knowledge of fundamental Data Management and thus poor data quality that will unnecessarily slow down, if not even endanger, the digital success of the company. So for enterprises, mastering the "Big four V's" is the first and most important step in preparing for the digital future.

> **Principle 2:** Data Governance creates complexity reduction to help the business manage data challenges.

If we look back again at the five levels of complexity in dealing with data, the scope and scale of the data challenge becomes apparent, but also the solution space: companies must concern themselves more with the content (description of reality) and the habitats of the data (IT systems and IT infrastructure). This engagement must

THE 5 LEVELS OF COMPLEXITY IN DEALING WITH DATA

5	NUMBER, VARIETY & SPEED
4	CORPORATE PROCESSES & LEGAL REQUIREMENTS
3	CONSISTENT DATA MAINTENANCE BY EMPLOYEES ALONG THE COMPANY PROCESSES
2	STABLE DATA QUALITY IN COMPLEX IT LANDSCAPES - INTEROPERABILITY
1	DESCRIPTION OF REALITY IN LINE WITH REQUIREMENTS

Fig. 2.5 The 5 levels of complexity in dealing with data in companies © Lars Michael Bollweg 2022. All Rights Reserved

take place within the framework of a professional data organization. And this data organization must work toward the company's goals. Why? Because we are generating more and more data in all areas of the company and depend on the quality of this data for the success of the company today and in the future. Professional Data Management creates the framework for this solution, and the company enforces Data Management with the help of Data Governance as the basis for the data organization and as the pacemaker for digital transformation (see Fig. 2.5).

2.3 Data Lifecycle

The great difficulty for companies to professionally manage data lies in the high complexity of the often very abstract topic "data." Each level of complexity in dealing with data is a challenge in itself. And the high complexity of the data challenges also explains why companies cannot be successful, or not successful enough, with a central Data Management department consisting of data analysts and database administrators alone. Data is created everywhere in the company; it accompanies every company process and contributes significantly to the company's success. An isolated, centralized view of data will not lead to the goal without including all levels, i.e., the requirements, systems, processes, and people in the company. Successful digital development therefore requires a more comprehensive implementation of Data Management in corporate processes. Data Governance is required along the entire data lifecycle (Soares 2015b).

Principle 3: Data Governance stands for holistic management of data along the entire data lifecycle.

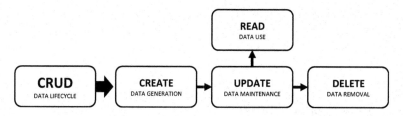

Fig. 2.6 The data lifecycle © Lars Michael Bollweg 2022. All Rights Reserved

The data lifecycle is often described in data science using the CRUD perspective. CRUD stands for "Create, Read, Update, and Delete" (see Fig. 2.6). CRUD thus describes the lifecycle of data using the major turning points in the life of data. It all starts with creation. Once the data has made it into the databases and systems, the use of the data comes into focus. Whether data is used by people or systems, the CRUD perspective does not care for now. Each type of use is documented in a non-discriminatory manner. Following the use, the change of the data is considered by the CRUD perspective: Who is responsible for data maintenance? What processes are lived here? The CRUD perspective, and with it the data lifecycle, concludes with the final termination of the data, the data deletion.

If you track the history of data on the basis of these important milestones (CRUD perspective), you can trace the life of data in a process-oriented manner. Accordingly, data can also be managed in a data process-oriented manner. Along the observation of the data process, the company finds answers to following questions: What errors occurred during the generation of the data? Does the generation of the data match the requirements of its use? How is data maintenance monitored and controlled? Is it ensured that the data still fits the requirement after maintenance? And finally, is the data deleted only when it should be deleted? Or even the answer to the question whether the data has been deleted at all?

The CRUD perspective shows Data Management the path of the data in the company and thus enables communication to be transferred from the pure description of the point level (this data is in the form "A" in the database "B") to a process level (this data is created at time "A" for the purpose "B" and is changed over time by the employee "C" and then deleted at the end of the process at time "X" in accordance with the specifications).

Developing and operationalizing the CRUD perspective requires that Data Management is not seen in isolation from the company's processes (and is not only included in a problem-related manner or only responding to the most pressing data problems), but is integrated into the organization of the company's processes. The integration of Data Management as a craft and corporate function into the company's process-based workflows is also the decisive factor in supporting digital value creation within the company in a process-oriented manner. Data Management must therefore become part of the organizational structure and the process organization in order to fully exploit its potential.

So it is no surprise that sensibly planned Data Governance should also be part of the structural and process organization in order to carry Data Management practices into the company and into the business departments.

2.4   Data Responsibility

Data Governance enables a company to communicate and make decisions regarding data and all other data-driven issues within an organization. The ability to communicate is ensured by linking Data Management with the company processes (the organizational chart around data with a view on the data lifecycle). The company becomes capable of making decisions by assigning responsibility for data—the data ownership (Seiner 2014).

> **Principle 4:** Data responsibility is the organizational solution to the complex coordination challenges that arise from the high interconnectedness of data flows within an organization.

Cooperation and coordination always lead to conflicts of interest of one kind or another. This is the normal case in other subject areas as well, but is part of day-to-day business, especially when it comes to issues surrounding data. Usually, competing interests and the often resulting standstill in a company are resolved by a clear hierarchy and clear corporate goals. If two employees disagree on the design and elaboration of a task, they turn to their manager, who ideally breaks the stalemate thus created and gets the company moving again. In the case of data, however, the escalation paths in companies are not clarified in most cases. Who makes the decision? Who needs to be asked at all? This unresolved organizational situation usually leads to long waiting times and often to "political" rather than sensible solutions.

In order to avoid standstills and waiting times in the face of data challenges and to enable continuous further development, it is important to clarify the issue of data responsibility clearly and transparently for everyone within the organization. What sounds simple, however, presents most companies with major problems: companies are repeatedly faced with the question of how a meaningful allocation of data responsibility can be implemented in practice.

In companies, one usually finds three concepts for the assignment of data responsibility: (1) political assignment, (2) functional assignment, and the (3) structural assignment.

(1) **Political Assignment of Data Responsibility:**
   The "political approach" assigns responsibility for data "freely" based on areas of interest and business responsibility. That is, if a leader within the leadership is particularly committed to or interested in the responsibility of a particular data

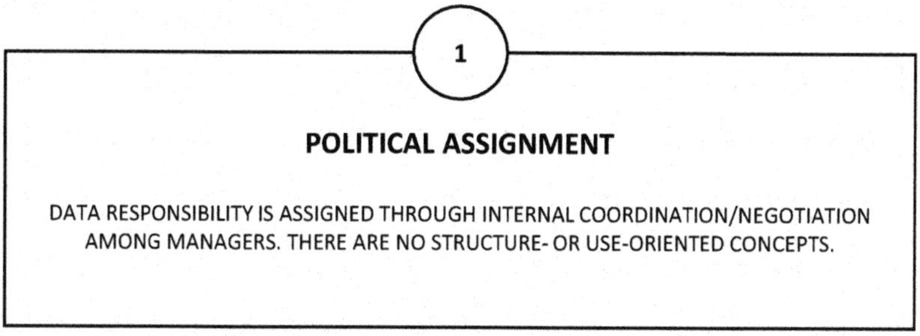

POLITICAL ASSIGNMENT

DATA RESPONSIBILITY IS ASSIGNED THROUGH INTERNAL COORDINATION/NEGOTIATION
AMONG MANAGERS. THERE ARE NO STRUCTURE- OR USE-ORIENTED CONCEPTS.

Fig. 2.7 Political assignment of data responsibility © Lars Michael Bollweg 2022. All Rights Reserved

FUNCTIONAL ASSIGNMENT

DATA RESPONSIBILITY IS ASSIGNED ACCORDING TO SPECIALIST TOPICS. THERE ARE NO
USAGE-ORIENTED CONCEPTS.

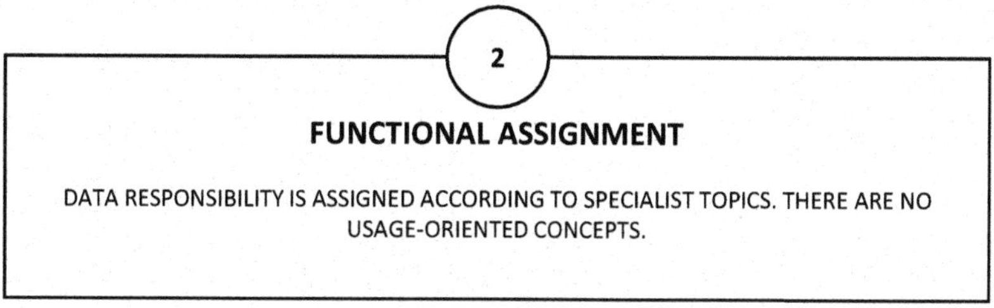

Fig. 2.8 Functional assignment of data responsibility © Lars Michael Bollweg 2022. All Rights Reserved

topic and prevails with his or her interest, then that leader is assigned responsibility for that data without further investigation of capabilities or dependencies (see Fig. 2.7).

(2) **Functional Assignment of Data Responsibility:**
The "functional approach" assigns data responsibility on the basis of functional responsibilities. This means that data responsibility, e.g., for material master data, is also assigned to the person who has functional responsibility for the materials. The focus on functional responsibility is important in this approach. In the "functional approach," data responsibility is not necessarily assigned to a manager. In fact, the opposite is often the case in practice. The assignment of functional responsibility is usually found in the line (organizational structure) (see Fig. 2.8).

(3) **Structural Assignment of Data Responsibility:**
The "structural approach" assigns data responsibility according to clear principles of use. The best known of these is the "creator principle." This principle states that the business unit that generates (creates) the data is also responsible for the data. However, other structure-related principles are also conceivable for structural allocation. The "maintainer principle," for example, states that the area that maintains the data is responsible for the data. In the structural assignment of data responsibility, responsibility is usually assigned to managers with budget and line responsibility (see Fig. 2.9).

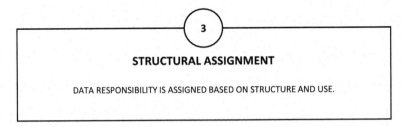

Fig. 2.9 Structural assignment of data responsibility © Lars Michael Bollweg 2022. All Rights Reserved

Of course, other approaches to assignment are conceivable, e.g., variations or combination models. In practice, however, these three approaches dominate and thus form a good starting point.

Let's therefore briefly classify the three established approaches a little further:

A free or political assignment of responsibility (whoever feels responsible for a data set raises their hand) poses organizational and human challenges within organizations and companies. Organizational challenges because, in the case of a political assignment, it is not always clear to employees who in the company is now responsible for which data and likewise where their responsibility ends. Human challenges, because in a freely designed system of responsibilities, the structure of the data organization is a constant plaything of shifts in power and responsibility. Politically very successful executives in particular develop themselves and their careers very quickly and also change their thematic interests with each internal promotion. This means that a political approach only rarely has the necessary stability to successfully implement a data organization in the long term.

In contrast to the political variant, which is obviously not at all recommendable, the functional assignment of data responsibility at least has strengths and weaknesses. In any case, the strength of this assignment is that it can be established in the company without major resistance, since employees who already have functional or operational responsibility for a topic can also understand the assigned data responsibility. Frequently, poor data quality in the areas of responsibility of these operational employees creates acute problems, which is why they even actively seek and want to hold this responsibility. There is also less movement in positions of functional responsibility, so organizational stability is rarely threatened. Despite these undisputed strengths, the functional assignment of data responsibility has a decisive disadvantage: employees with functional responsibility are usually not sufficiently empowered to make decisions. In other words, they lack the authority to truly manage data. As a result of the low location of responsibility in the line, the functional assignment often requires much more unnecessary coordination and persuasion in order to enforce decisions with consequences in the line or in the budget. In view of these obvious organizational deficiencies, one often hears the statement that if one assigns data responsibility to an employee, one must also enable this employee to fulfill this responsibility at the same time. In other words, the technical assignment of data responsibility fails more often due to the organization's

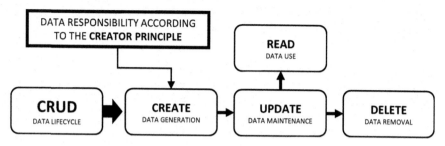

Fig. 2.10 The creator principle © Lars Michael Bollweg 2022. All Rights Reserved

lack of decision-making capacity and the usually not clearly defined escalation paths for decision-making than due to the commitment and motivation of the employees themselves.

The structural assignment of data responsibility is different. It overcomes the limitations of political and functional allocation by clearly mapping organizational lines of responsibility, created by unambiguous principles. The creator principle has become established here, which is why the assignment of data responsibility along this principle will be discussed in more detail below (see Fig. 2.10).

Principle 5: Data responsibility is assigned according to the creator principle.

Data responsibility according to the creator principle is based on the CRUD data lifecycle. Whenever data is generated within an organization, data responsibility for the entire subsequent data lifecycle lies with the generating (creating) area and its management.

Misconceptions quickly arise, especially when it comes to questions about data responsibility, so it should be emphasized here that although an individual employee generates individual data, e.g., enters data, and is of course responsible for his or her own work and the quality of his or her input, data responsibility in the sense of Data Governance should not be understood as individual responsibility, but as departmental responsibility. The concept of data responsibility must be viewed in the context of establishing and expanding the data organization through Data Governance. Data responsibility is the basis of the data organization or, in other words, the data organization emerges and operates along the structures of data responsibility.

Assigning responsibility for data according to the creator principle is a top management and leadership issue and should therefore be placed with managers with personnel and budget responsibility. This follows the conviction that only those who are also in a position to assume responsibility can be responsible. A clerk may be responsible for his or her own input of data, but he or she cannot oversee the flow of information within an organization and certainly cannot influence the handling of data within the company through personnel or budget decisions and thus ensure good data quality.

Principle 6: Data responsibility lies with top management.

The importance of data responsibility and the significance of the decision in favor of one of the approaches presented for assigning data responsibility and their crucial role for the success of Data Governance should have become clear by this point. Data responsibility creates the basis for the role-based data organization that is to be implemented in the company as part of Data Governance. And, to use the statements from the beginning of this chapter once again: data responsibility creates the basis for the organizational chart around data and data responsibility structures the listed areas. So with the assignment of data responsibility, we create the mapping of the organizational structures in the org chart. However, these organizational structures still need to be further filled with life. The further assignments to the required roles that are still necessary are shown and discussed in the following chapter.

2.5   Roles of Data Governance

To implement and operationalize data responsibility and thus ensure professional handling of data within a company, Data Governance implements a role-based virtual organization within the company (Seiner 2014; Madsen 2019).

Principle 7: Data Governance is a role-based form of organization.

This means that meaningful Data Governance does not organize and ensure the handling (creation, use, maintenance, deletion) of data solely via a central department, e.g., Data Management, but rather in a decentralized manner with the help of the integration of Data Management into the business units. On the one hand, this means that Data Management employees move into the departments and work together with the departments on solutions to data challenges. But it also means that the task profiles of line employees within the departments are expanded to include new tasks and roles, namely the tasks and roles within Data Governance.

A role-based data organization ensures two things:

On the one hand, the data challenges that arise decentrally are also managed and solved decentrally. Today, a central organization is generally no longer able to cope with the multitude of decentrally emerging challenges. For a centralized entity, data problems are like a hydra; cut off the head of one problem and two new ones emerge. Data problems have to be tackled at their source, i.e., at data generation in the business units, in order to solve them in the long term.

On the other hand, the data organization remains lean through the assignment of roles in the departments and becomes capable of action. For solving data problems, the role-based data organization creates a powerful structure that does not require the addition of new, untrained employees. The key to success is empowering existing staff and using Data Management as a multiplier for data expertise. The only alternative to empowering existing staff is to build new staff. In fact, as a general rule, a company today no longer has a choice about whether or not to solve its data problems. It only has the choice of how. However, hiring and training new staff to take over data maintenance and data cleansing is very costly and time-consuming. These are costs and time that the company usually does not have to invest, since it usually already has data experts in the company. These data experts are the employees who already create, use, maintain, and delete the data today. These employees only need to be organized via Data Governance, provided with the right assignments and procedures, and enabled to handle data professionally via continuing education and training.

But be careful when developing a role-based organization that is placed on top of the day-to-day business of an existing process organization. Particularly in large companies, there is a risk that role-based organizational forms will overload employees with tasks and responsibilities to or beyond their limit. This role overload must be avoided by management and executives and the workload of employees must be consciously controlled. Nevertheless, it is unfortunately not an option for executives to simply block off the task of "Data Management." Especially in the case of data challenges, there is simply no way for modern companies not to fulfill this task, since the company's success depends more and more on professionally managed data from week to week, from project to project, from further development to further development.

The solution to this conflict of goals lies in role inclusion.

> **Principle 8:** Role inclusion is one of the fundamentals of organizational planning for Data Governance and states that management should identify employees to participate in Data Governance who have also managed the data prior to the implementation of Data Governance.

Role inclusion looks for the "existing data experts" in the company, who are usually already present in all departments today. These data experts have just never been mandated by an official role and job description for this activity. Finding this meaningful link between role and personnel is the core task of executives in building and implementing Data Governance. After all, only role inclusion fully exploits all the advantages and existing synergy effects in the company. And only with the help of role inclusion can companies ensure that data is managed in a future-proof manner, interoperability is promoted, and the line is not overloaded at the same time.

In Data Governance, there are usefully the following five roles: (1) the data owner, (2) the data steward, (3) the subject matter expert, (4) the data project manager, and (5) the IT administrator. In the following, we look at the Data Governance roles in detail (see Fig. 2.11):

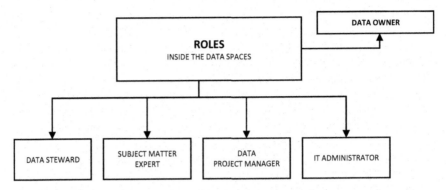

Fig. 2.11 The roles of data governance © Lars Michael Bollweg 2022. All Rights Reserved

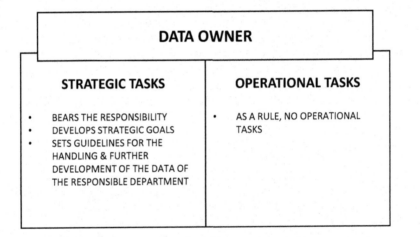

Fig. 2.12 Data owner role © Lars Michael Bollweg 2022. All Rights Reserved

(1) Data Owner

The Data Owner role is filled by a senior executive in top management—usually one reporting level below C-level. The role holds the responsibility for the data that is generated in the respective responsible area of the senior executive. The data owner role is not an operational role in handling data, but a strategic one. The data owner develops strategic goals and sets guidelines for the handling and further development of data in his or her area. Operational staff are accountable to the data owner. The data owner is the most important and at the same time the last step on the escalation path if there are discrepancies in the handling of data in his or her area or in coordination with other areas. The data owner ensures the organizational ability to act and make decisions about data (see Fig. 2.12).

DATA STEWARD	
STRATEGIC TASKS	**OPERATIONAL TASKS**
• PROVIDES IMPETUS FOR STRATEGIC SPECIFICATIONS / DEVELOPMENTS TO THE DATA OWNER	• COORDINATES DATA PROJECTS • ENABLES THE DEPARTMENT TO EFFICIENTLY AND SUCCESSFULLY IMPLEMENT DATA PROJECTS • ENSURES THAT DATA MANAGEMENT PRACTICES ARE IMPLEMENTED

Fig. 2.13 Data steward role © Lars Michael Bollweg 2022. All Rights Reserved

(2) Data Steward

In addition to the strategic role of the data owner, a company also needs an operational role that operationally implements the strategic directives of the data owner and coordinates the resulting data development projects. This is the task of the "data steward." The data steward is a specialist role. The role is designed to be a dual multiplier. On the one hand, the data steward ensures that the necessary expertise from the specialist areas flows into the implementation of data projects and that these projects are aligned with concrete pain points in the organization. On the other hand, he or she ensures that the practices of Data Management are also transferred into the daily work of the departments by exemplifying and demanding these practices as "primus inter pares," as a "first among equals."

The role of the data steward is most appropriately hung along the matrix organization of a company, as the potential synergies and efficiencies leveraged by Data Management are most effective along company processes. The data steward is typically a new role for a company and one for which the company must allocate appropriate time resources to an employee to fulfill. In the rarest of cases, however, the data steward role is a full-time position (see Fig. 2.13).

(3) Subject Matter Expert

Even the most qualified data steward is not able to have all the details about all the data in his head. On his own, he simply cannot keep track of all the realities summarized in data in the complex day-to-day business of a company. Therefore, in many cases, he or she is dependent on the advice of technical and factual data experts. These business and technical data experts are usually senior employees of the business departments or IT departments with many years of experience in dealing with data as well as with the realities and technicalities that this data describes. The role of a subject matter expert is purely advisory. Only in rare cases

```
┌─────────────────────────────────────────────────────────┐
│                 SUBJECT MATTER EXPERT                     │
└─────────────────────────────────────────────────────────┘
┌──────────────────────────┬──────────────────────────────┐
│     STRATEGIC TASKS      │      OPERATIONAL TASKS         │
│                          │                                │
│  •  PROVIDES IMPETUS FOR │  •  ADVISES THE DATA STEWARD   │
│     STRATEGIC            │  •  IN RARE CASES, ALSO WORKS  │
│     SPECIFICATIONS /     │     OPERATIONALLY ON DATA      │
│     DEVELOPMENTS TO THE  │     PROJECTS                   │
│     DATA STEWARD AND THE │                                │
│     DATA OWNER           │                                │
│                          │                                │
└──────────────────────────┴──────────────────────────────┘
```

Fig. 2.14 Subject matter expert role © Lars Michael Bollweg 2022. All Rights Reserved

are these experts entrusted with specific tasks in operational projects that go beyond consulting. Since the data experts can perform this consulting role without much effort as part of their normal work, no extra time resources are required for this role. However, even if this role only has an advisory function, the subject matter experts should be documented by name within Data Governance (keyword: data-related organizational chart) so that the relevant contact persons are already known in the event of questions or problems with specific data and time-consuming research work and waiting times can be saved (see Fig. 2.14).

(4) Data Project Manager
The data project manager role is an operational role that is usually filled by a data expert (data analyst, database administrator, data engineer, etc.) from a Data Management department. While all of the roles mentioned so far have a strong connection to the business unit and tend to involve higher-level content-related or coordinating tasks, the data project manager is the role that ensures that data within data projects can be prepared and developed appropriately. The employee who fills this role is usually in a position to evaluate and monitor data quality and, if action is required, to independently perform data cleansing and further data transformations. Typically, an employee performing this role will have a good working knowledge of a programming language, such as Python, and will be able to query databases, e.g., using SQL. Of course, in order to use such a role, there must be a corresponding qualified employee within the Data Management department. If your company does not have the appropriate personnel, then in this case you should put this book aside for a while if necessary and begin to hire appropriate personnel and first begin to build up a professional Data Management department. After all, only when the company has built up qualified resources in the "data space" it can work on putting them to good use. Without a data project manager, professional Data Management and thus the establishment of Data Governance are not possible. One can only repeat

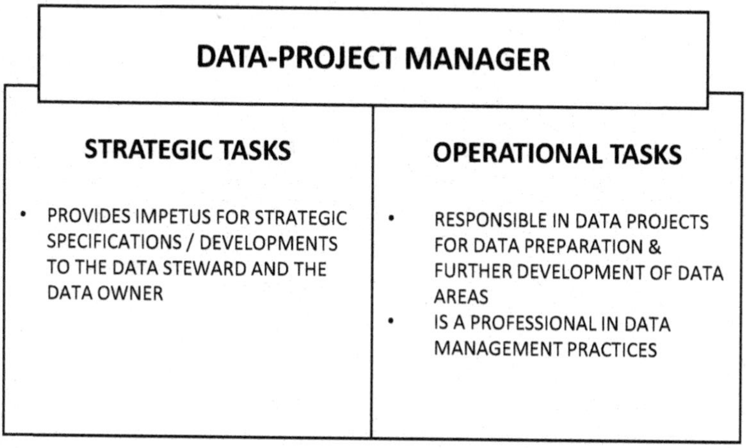

Fig. 2.15 Data project manager role © Lars Michael Bollweg 2022. All Rights Reserved

it again and again. Data Management is not a "sideline activity" that the business department can carry out on its own without further qualification. It is a specialist area with high training requirements in order to reach a professional level (see Fig. 2.15).

(5) IT Administrator

The final role within Data Governance is the role of the IT administrator. In addition to the coordination of projects and requirements by the data steward, consulting by the subject matter experts, and data preparation and processing by the data project manager, there is usually still a need for a role that is also capable of implementing desired changes in the respective systems in order to successfully complete data projects. The role of the IT administrator can be performed by both internal system managers and external service providers. The IT administrator role is usually already filled within the company and also requires no further allocation of time resources. But similar to the subject matter experts, documentation by Data Governance is also necessary here in order to quickly get to the appropriate contact person in case of questions or problems. In addition, it makes sense to involve the IT administrator as early as possible in data projects, as this role can supplement the often existing knowledge about processes and data with knowledge about the system and application. In this way, data project teams receive early indications of any pitfalls or special features that may arise from the system or database architecture (see Fig. 2.16).

Looking at the individual roles of Data Governance within a RASCI matrix (Responsible, Accountable, Support, Consulted, Informed) results in the role classification shown in Fig. 2.17. An abbreviated version of the role descriptions can be found in Fig. 2.18.

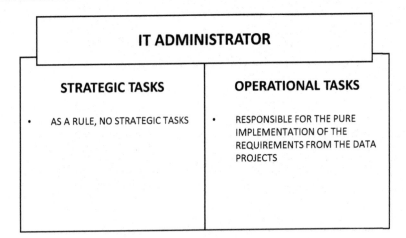

Fig. 2.16 IT administrator role © Lars Michael Bollweg 2022. All Rights Reserved

DATA OWNER	DATA STEWARD	SUBJECT MATTER EXPERT	DATA-PROJECT MANAGER	IT ADMINISTRATOR
ACCOUNTABLE	RESPONSIBLE	CONSULTED	SUPPORT	SUPPORT

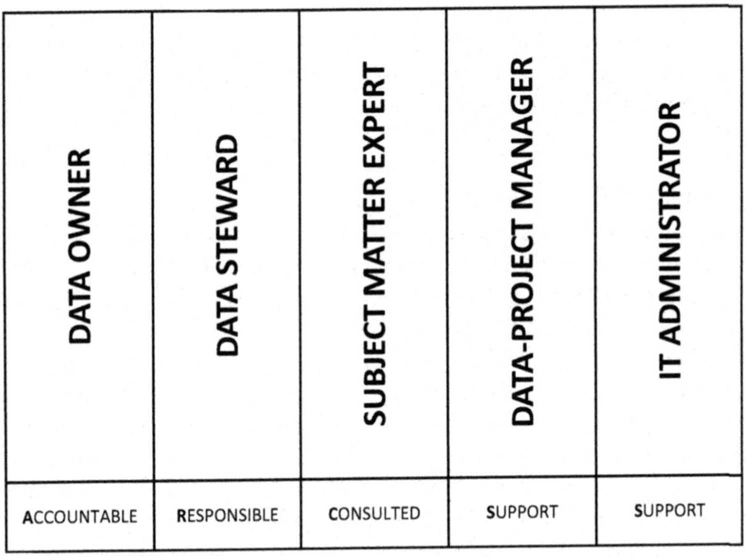

Fig. 2.17 RASCI matrix allocation of Data Governance roles © Lars Michael Bollweg 2022. All Rights Reserved

It is also important to note once again the origin of the respective roles. While the data stewards and the subject matter experts are usually business departmental roles, the data project manager and the IT administrator usually come from the departmental support units in the IT departments. This parity of business and IT units clearly shows that successful Data Management within Data Governance can only be achieved with business and IT integration. Neither side is capable of successfully

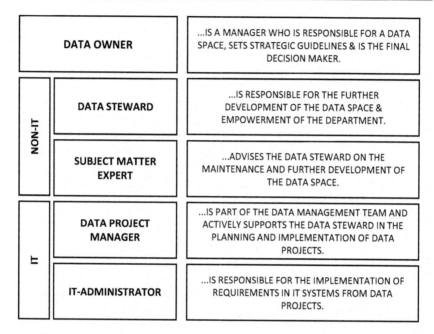

	DATA OWNER	...IS A MANAGER WHO IS RESPONSIBLE FOR A DATA SPACE, SETS STRATEGIC GUIDELINES & IS THE FINAL DECISION MAKER.
NON-IT	DATA STEWARD	...IS RESPONSIBLE FOR THE FURTHER DEVELOPMENT OF THE DATA SPACE & EMPOWERMENT OF THE DEPARTMENT.
NON-IT	SUBJECT MATTER EXPERT	...ADVISES THE DATA STEWARD ON THE MAINTENANCE AND FURTHER DEVELOPMENT OF THE DATA SPACE.
IT	DATA PROJECT MANAGER	...IS PART OF THE DATA MANAGEMENT TEAM AND ACTIVELY SUPPORTS THE DATA STEWARD IN THE PLANNING AND IMPLEMENTATION OF DATA PROJECTS.
IT	IT-ADMINISTRATOR	...IS RESPONSIBLE FOR THE IMPLEMENTATION OF REQUIREMENTS IN IT SYSTEMS FROM DATA PROJECTS.

Fig. 2.18 Summary of Data Governance roles © Lars Michael Bollweg 2022. All Rights Reserved

implementing data projects by itself. Solving data challenges is therefore not a purely departmental or purely IT task. Solving data challenges is an enterprise task.

> **Principle 9:** The roles of Data Governance should be filled equally by the business units and the IT-related departments. Data Governance is a driver for business and IT integration.

As a final addition to the roles presented, it is important to emphasize once again that the tailoring of the role-based organization of Data Governance discussed here enables the fastest path to professional Data Management within an organization. The role-based organization of Data Governance takes into account all the necessary capabilities and places a strong emphasis on the involvement of business units in Data Management. At the same time, the primary goal remains to make the introduction of Data Governance as low effort as possible for the respective company while still significantly improving the ability to act when dealing with data. The implementation of Data Governance follows the philosophy that first the tasks for managing data that are already performed by employees in the company (role inclusion) are transferred into organizational structures of Data Governance. And, that these structures are gradually professionalized in a second step by introducing the practices of Data Management and the associated empowerment of employees in dealing with data. Managers entrusted with setting up Data Governance are therefore well advised to look intensively for the employees who already perform the data maintenance and data management tasks in the company today. In this way, synergies and efficiencies can be leveraged for the company and, at the same time, barriers to implementation and recruitment can be removed.

At the end of this section, one last note, and yes, this is a repeat: Despite this noble goal of generating as little effort as possible in the existing organization, it must also be noted again and again that professional Data Management is not a "side job" and cannot be realized without appropriately trained personnel with time resources. But it should also be emphasized again: Few investments that a company makes in this day and age have as lasting and positive an effect on the company's success as professional Data Management. All the more so when it comes to the digital transformation of companies for the future.

2.6   Structures of Data Governance

Now that we have created the structures in the organizational chart around data with the help of data responsibility and supplemented these organizational structures with the roles of Data Governance, it is time to turn to the structures of Data Governance themselves. The Data Governance structures provide the organizational framework within which the roles perform their tasks and cooperate with each other. They again overlay the Data Governance structures and enable cooperation and coordination in the data organization. In Data Governance, there are six organizational structures that together guide the operational and strategic development of data in the enterprise (Ladley 2012; Templar 2017): (1) corporate data spaces and the data space organization, (2) corporate core processes/department organization, (3) data project teams, (4) Data Governance office, (5) Council of Data Stewards, and (6) Council of Data Owners (see Fig. 2.19).

Corporate Data Spaces and Data Space Organization
At the lowest and most granular level of data organization, we find the corporate data spaces of a company. For many, the data space logic appears at first glance to be yet another abstract entity. But in fact the data space logic is simple and catchy. Just have a little patience.

Let's start with a brief definition and then go deeper into the topic with the help of examples:

▶ A corporate data space represents a collection of physical data and data tables in systems and databases for which a data owner is responsible.

The corporate data space is therefore the sphere of action of the data owner in the data organization. As a rule, the data within a corporate data space is logically and thematically related. If a data owner is responsible for two or three completely different data topics that can be meaningfully separated from one another, it is possible to assign two or three corporate data spaces to one data owner without

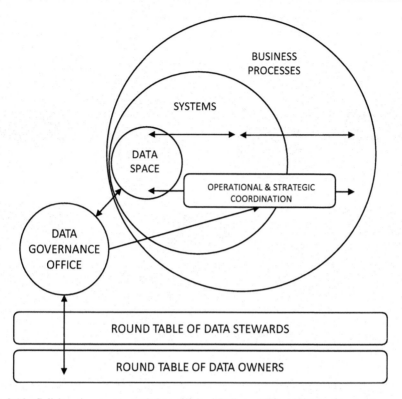

Fig. 2.19 Collaboration structures © Lars Michael Bollweg 2022. All Rights Reserved

any problems. However, it is important to assign Data Governance roles for each of these corporate data spaces. But again, it is usually not a problem if one employee is the data steward for two or three data spaces at the same time.

Data spaces are usually cut along logical connections of the data. The term "tailoring" is appropriate because every company can freely design its data spaces, i.e., tailor them individually. The logical context within a corporate data space is usually mapped with the help of so-called data domains (see Fig. 2.20).

Data domains are nothing but data categories, i.e., certain groups of data, for which because of their interrelated and related essence core, joint support, joint management makes sense. Corporate data spaces and data domains can be thought of as two hierarchical levels of data. At the top level of the hierarchy, you find the corporate data space, and at the level below that, the level of the domain. Theoretically, it would be conceivable to subdivide this hierarchy even further. For example, to subdivide data domains with sub-data domains. In practice, however, i.e., in the everyday work of companies, further subdivision is seldom necessary and even less useful.

As already mentioned, the concept of corporate data spaces and data domains seems very abstract to many at first glance. However, it loses its abstractness very quickly when we discuss a few examples of this:

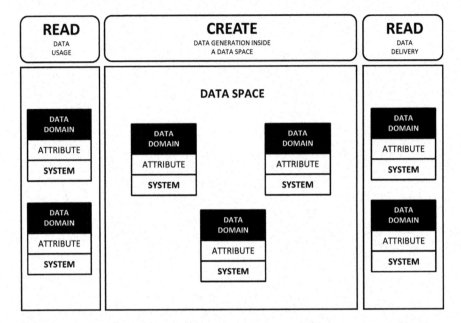

Fig. 2.20 Corporate data space mapping with data domains © Lars Michael Bollweg 2022. All Rights Reserved

---

Example

Let's take, for example, a department in charge of designing and building houses. For the data that is generated in this department, there are different possibilities to split it into data spaces. For example, a commonly chosen layout would be to create a single "Design and Build" data space. In this one data space all data of the department is comprised.

But let's assume that the department is very large and that two trades work hand in hand within the department. On the one hand, there are the planners, who plan the construction in detail, and on the other hand, there are the craftsmen, who realize the construction on the construction site. It can therefore make sense to set a further dividing line along these trades and to cut two data spaces. One data space "planning data" and a second data space, e.g., "construction documentation data." ◄

The service that corporate data spaces provide in the company is simple but effective; they create an organizational framework to which the company can assign data responsibility. Data spaces accomplish this by aggregating the data generated in an area, e.g., a department, into a data space. Again, the keyword here is complexity reduction. With the help of data spaces, employees in a company become capable of speaking, who otherwise fall silent before the flood of data elements and data

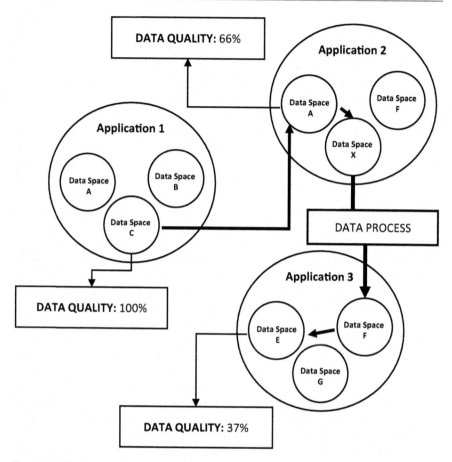

Fig. 2.21 The Data process map © Lars Michael Bollweg 2022. All Rights Reserved

holding systems. With the help of data spaces, every employee in the company knows which data is managed, created, used, maintained, and deleted where and by whom. So also who to talk to if there are data problems within this group of data.

The boundaries for the scope of a data space are set by the data owner. Data spaces form the operational framework of data responsibility and thus the framework for the professional management of data. The structures of Data Governance are therefore based on the content of the data (data domain) and the areas of responsibility of the executives, the data owners, in top management.

The data generated in the manager's area of responsibility together forms the corporate data spaces for which the manager is responsible. Whether this data space is subdivided again or managed operationally within an organizational structure lies within the degrees of freedom that good Data Governance leaves to the department.

With the help of data spaces, the image of an organization chart around data, which has already been used frequently, can also be realized graphically (see Fig. 2.21). Data Governance based on data domains creates a data structure and data process map that shows which data from which data space is located in which system. Of course, this also shows which data steward is responsible for which data space and who the responsible data owner for this data space is.

Principle 10: Data sets are structured and comprised in corporate data spaces.

But the data structure and data process map shows even more. It makes the data processes between the individual systems visible and thus enables process-oriented management of the data. This process-oriented view of the data gives the company and its managers completely new possibilities for intervention in the management of the data, e.g., for managing data quality. Without a view of the data process, data quality can only be optimized selectively, i.e., within a database. Only the process-oriented view makes it possible to optimize the entire data chain. And ideally, this should already be done at the point where the data is generated, since there is no more favorable place for optimizing data than at the beginning of the data process. Any optimization in downstream systems amounts to a second touch, a double work. Optimization at the source is always the most organizationally favorable time and should always be the starting point for all data quality optimization measures.

So if you look at a data process with three stations in three systems, you often see the following picture. At the first station, i.e., in the system that generates the data, the data quality is still at a high level, e.g., at 100%. This means that the data requirements of the first system are met 100% by the data generation. This is often the case because the generation system is designed to serve the data requirements of the first station. The dialogs fit the requirements and the data structures fit the dialogs. But often the picture changes when another system is added at a second station that has different requirements for the data. Then the data quality, which was still unproblematic in the source system, suddenly reaches a critical level, e.g., 66%. Only 66% of the data fit the data requirements of the second station. And when a third station is added to the chain, the data quality often drops even further. And the data that fit so well for the first system in the first station drops to another low, e.g., 37%.

In a non-process-oriented Data Management system, system administrators and data managers would now carry out isolated data optimization measures at each station and, in extreme cases, adapt and optimize the same data set three times to the three different data requirements. A process-oriented view of the data and information flows along the structures of Data Governance makes it possible to optimize the data once for all the requirements of the data process, and it makes sense to do this at the point where the data is generated, i.e., in the source system at station one.

Data Governance based on corporate data spaces and the necessary roles creates new opportunities for management to not only manage data more professionally, but also to do so more economically and efficiently.

However, these are not all the intervention options that corporate data spaces and Data Governance enable a company to have. In addition to the optimization of data

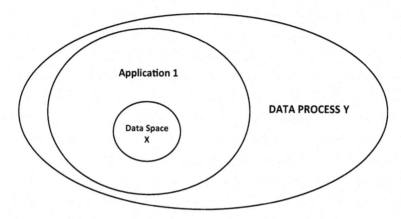

Fig. 2.22 Data space logic—first case class © Lars Michael Bollweg 2022. All Rights Reserved

qualities, completely new perspectives also arise for the company. For example, the examination of data, data quality, and the associated data requirements shows very well in which areas of the data structure and data process map a company is particularly innovative in the utilization of data, i.e., where it is constantly making new demands on the data. And on the contrary, of course, where this is not the case. The systems and data where the company has not developed further for a long time become visible. If necessary, the management should take a closer look at these areas in order to drive development around the data again.

The same view becomes possible via the assignment of the Data Governance roles to the personnel. The data structure and data process map with the documentation of the Data Governance roles clearly shows for which data there are sufficient technical and factual data experts in the company and, of course, again the opposite. It quickly becomes apparent in which departments the data knowledge in the company is distributed over too few shoulders and for which topics the management should also send another employee for training, if necessary, in order to be able to compensate for possible absences or unexpected departures.

Data Governance therefore opens up much more than just a view of the data for the company. Data Governance enables a new view of the handling of data (innovation), transparency along the usage of data (data requirements), and the associated staff (data organization and competence clusters).

Now that data spaces have hopefully lost their abstract character and the idea of what a data space is and how it is tailored has been sharpened, all that is missing is a clear understanding of how data spaces behave in interaction with the other layers, consisting of processes and systems, and what rules they are subject to.

The logic of the data spaces is also very simple here, but one must visualize the structures one more time with the help of an example of different case classes.

The simplest case looks like this: A corporate data space describes all data of a system and the system serves a single business process (see Fig. 2.22).

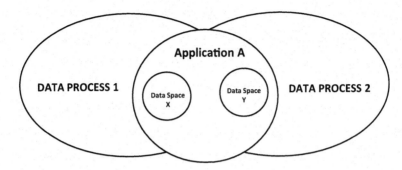

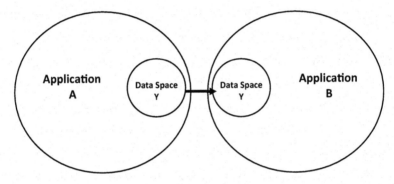

Unfortunately, the reality in our companies is not that simple, so a little more flexibility is needed here.

A more complex case could therefore also look like this: A corporate data space under the responsibility of data owner X and another corporate data space under the responsibility of data owner Y jointly describe all data in system A. The data space of X serves to fulfill enterprise process 1 and the data space of Y serves to fulfill enterprise process 2 (see Fig. 2.23).

An increase of the complexity is still possible: A corporate data space of the responsible person V describes the data in system A and by the data transfer over an interface likewise the data in system B (see Fig. 2.24).

The case classes listed illustrate once again the flexibility of the data space logic for the development of a data organization. This flexibility in the design of the "organizational chart around data," i.e., in the design of the data structure and data process map, makes it possible to map and transparently display the data and data responsibilities of the entire company.

Since an understanding of data space logic is of crucial importance for the subsequent success of Data Governance, we bring together all the points already mentioned once again below: The structure of the data spaces alone makes the central importance of the data space logic for Data Governance visible. However, the structure only forms the framework that the content really fills with life. For a better understanding of the data space organization, it is necessary to visualize the roles of Data Governance again. For the data space organization, the data owner and the data steward are of decisive importance.

As an executive, the data owner is usually entrusted with personnel and budget responsibility at a direct reporting level to the C-level management. These top management executives are usually no longer operationally involved in maintaining the data entrusted to them, but develop strategic goals based on the overarching data or corporate strategy and delegate operational coordination and implementation to a data steward.

> **Principle 11:** Data owners set strategic goals and delegate operational imple-mentation to data stewards.

The data steward takes over the operational data space organization for the data owner. In addition to prioritizing possible data projects, one of his or her main tasks is to design and document the corporate data spaces. The rule of thumb for the design of a data space is that a data steward can only coordinate a set of data that is manageable for him and ideally logically connected (e.g., data of a company process). It therefore makes no sense for companies to appoint just one data steward and one corporate data space for the entire company and hope for the best. Typically, this one lone data steward would not be able to meaningfully coordinate all data challenges and, instead of helping the business, would only become a problem-reinforcing "bottleneck."

It is therefore important to ensure that the data steward remains capable of acting and only manages and coordinates a manageable amount of data within a data space. How large this "manageable amount" is depends on many factors. One is the quality of the data. One person can reasonably manage more data of good quality and less data of poor quality. Furthermore it depends, for example, on the variance of the data. A person can manage very large amounts of uniform data, but less data with a high number of different characteristics of data. Consequently, this means that if the data is highly complex and there are a large number of data problems, there may be several data spaces within the responsibility of one data owner and a group of data stewards. Accordingly, the right tailoring of data spaces is a challenge that depends on many individual factors.

The layout of the first corporate data spaces must be started with a sense of proportion and gut feeling and must then be questioned and adjusted again and again by the data steward in the course of the operational activities of Data Governance. Even though this topic takes time and a certain dynamic in the design is normal, it is important that corporate data spaces are documented and presented transparently at all times, e.g., within a data catalog or in the data structure and data process map.

In addition to the documentation of data and data domains, the documentation of Data Governance roles is also an important building block in the data space organization. Often, the documentation of the roles is even more valuable for the company than the documentation of the individual data fields itself. This is because knowledge about the data fields is made available to the company via the documentation of the roles. The business and factual data experts are the key to this knowledge, since they can interpret the data fields and their description of reality.

This procedure of first identifying and documenting the knowledge carriers and only then diving into the depths of the data details is "best practice" in Data Governance and will also be discussed in greater depth in the next chapters. Building on the knowledge about data and the knowledge about the reality behind the data, the so-called data requirements, the data space organization starts to develop the data assets within data projects in terms of the business objectives. It does not do this alone, but in cooperation with the other structures of Data Governance.

Corporate Core Processes/Department Organization
The most sensible way to ensure that Data Governance works toward corporate goals is to integrate Data Governance into the corporate process or departmental organization (i.e., into the matrix or line organization). This integration ensures that Data Governance does not operate as an external unit alongside the process or departmental organization, but is integrated into the organizational teams. In addition to the structural advantages, such as a high degree of proximity to the specialist area, this deep integration of Data Management gives the respective executives further intervention and control options to ensure that Data Governance works in a goal-oriented manner.

A sensibly developed Data Governance is a service provider for the company and aims for serving the company's goals, so it is particularly important that the Data Governance prioritizes the right goals. It makes no sense for a company if Data Governance develops an alternative agenda to the corporate processes or specialist departments and pursues these in a detached and uncoordinated manner. The integration of Data Governance into the operational process and department structures is one of the most important success factors for not only successfully managing data-driven developments in the long term, but also driving them within the company.

> **Principle 12:** Data Governance is most effective as an integrative part of the operational process and business unit organization.

In addition to the right target development, integration into the corporate process or departmental organization has another major advantage: organizational complexity reduction. We have already discussed the five levels of complexity in dealing with data in detail. Integrating Data Governance into the higher-level operational organization is a sensible way to reduce the number of anchor points for Data Management at all these levels to what is absolutely necessary. Data and data challenges exist in all business units and departments. Running Data Governance without a structural filter (control via enterprise process or departmental organization) within a large organization often makes it impossible to manage the flood of unprioritized tasks. The data organization needs a wave breaker, an upstream structural organizational unit from the matrix or line organization, which ensures that the data organization remains lean and that the tasks and challenges are entered into Data Governance in a prioritized manner.

Principle 13: Data Governance develops a lean, structured organization consisting of data owners and corporate data spaces.

The simplicity of the organizational structures also pursues the goal of reducing the complexity of the challenges from a management perspective and making them capable of action and control. This means that sensibly designed Data Governance also actively uses its structures to offer connection, exchange, intervention, and control options for management.

These structures can be traced very well along the company process and departmental organization. An individual department can prioritize its data challenge independently and initiate processing. In reality, however, this department is not in an isolated environment. The opposite is more likely to be the case; departments find themselves in a closely interwoven network with other departments, in which the data and information flows are characterized by complex dependencies and must be coordinated with one another. This is where Data Governance (based on data space logic), integrated into the enterprise process and departmental organization, really blossoms. After all, the truly transformational power of Data Governance for a company comes from linking the simple structures of the data spaces together to solve highly complex challenges. The whole thing can be thought of in modular terms. If a company needs to solve a data problem that requires the involvement of several players, the interlinking of data spaces provides precisely the solution and coordination space required in the organization, which would otherwise have to be created individually with a great deal of research and coordination effort.

Principle 14: Data Governance enables process-oriented management of data challenges.

Data Governance and the data space organization enable an End2End view of the complete data flows and data processes through modular linking of the data responsibilities and their data spaces, even across area and responsibility boundaries. This form of ability to act, which is often new for companies, accelerates coordination processes and provides solution options for data challenges at a significantly higher speed (see Fig. 2.25).

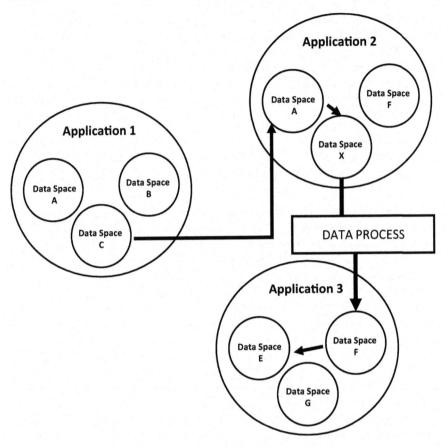

Fig. 2.25 Concatenation of corporate data spaces © Lars Michael Bollweg 2022. All Rights Reserved

Fig. 2.26 Differentiation of Data Governance from data projects © Lars Michael Bollweg 2022. All Rights Reserved

DATA GOVERNANCE	DATA PROJECTS
ORGANIZATION & DECISIONS	IMPLEMENTATION & SOLUTIONS

Data Project Teams

The data project teams are another important organizational structure. They are the key to the further development of data and data structures in the company. A topic that will come up again and again in the course of this book is the separation and distinction between the data organization aka Data Governance on the one hand and solving existing data problems in data projects on the other (see Fig. 2.26).

The structure of the data organization (Data Governance) is the basis for success-ful data projects, but in itself remains invisible to the company. This means that nothing has changed in the company with the establishment of a data organization alone. A lot of energy is invested, but no one sees results. Therefore, it is important to implement data projects (e.g., data quality cleansing, data research, interface descriptions, data request surveys, analyses and evaluations) directly in parallel with the setup of the data organization. These data projects should generally be implemented by individually assembled data project teams and staffed through Data Governance roles. This does not mean that all roles documented in Data Governance always work together for every data challenge, but rather that only the roles needed to meet a project goal ever come together in a data project team. Typically, the data steward coordinates the "staffing" of the data project teams and makes sure that he or she has all the necessary skills united in the respective data project team. The actual project management is then taken over by the data project manager, who is opera-tionally responsible for the implementation of the data project. It can also be said that the data steward ensures that the technical skills, i.e., the knowledge of the reality behind the data, are meaningfully represented in the project team, while the data project manager ensures that the implementation skills (the so-called technical skills) in the project team match the task. Because only together and in fusion of both perspectives, business and technical, can a data project be led to success by a project team.

The flexibility in the composition of a data project team makes it possible within Data Governance to map the interlinking of the data spaces in terms of personnel as well. For example, it is advisable to have data projects that include data that is highly significant for two data spaces implemented jointly by the two respective data project managers of the data spaces involved. In this way, in addition to the greatest possible security that all data requirements are implemented, the reporting and reporting level is also covered at the same time, since both data project managers report on the status of the data project within the data space and company process organization, for example.

Data Governance Office
To ensure that the Data Governance program achieves the desired results, it makes sense to establish a Data Governance office. The Data Governance office is the heart of the Data Governance program. It ensures that the implementation of Data Governance progresses and that the implementation of data projects stays on track.

On the one hand, the Data Governance office, i.e., the project management office, is responsible for Data Governance implementation. It is responsible for developing the implementation plan and tracking the implementation status. It handles the overarching communication with the departments and business units to ensure the necessary support for the introduction of Data Governance in the long term. Change management skills are as necessary in the Data Governance office as Data Manage-ment skills.

On the other hand, the Data Governance office sets the pace for operational work within the data spaces. It monitors the necessary documentation and ensures the networking of the individual data spaces and the quality of the implementation of the data projects.

In addition, the Data Governance office is entrusted with permanently working on improving the process model within Data Governance and enabling employees to implement the process model by offering further training and education.

Data Governance must implement all of these activities in line with the data strategy and business objectives.

In many cases, filling the Data Governance office marks the beginning of implementing Data Governance in the company. When appointing a Data Officer, therefore, much more attention must be paid to the employee's communication skills than to pure data skills. Combination models consisting of an employee with strong communication skills and an employee with strong technical skills can also be effective, since it is not always possible to find both in one person.

Round Table of Data Stewards
In a regular cycle, e.g., every three or every six months, all data stewards are called together in the Round Table of Data Stewards to come together for an overarching exchange. Topics such as changes in the data strategy, new legal requirements for data protection and data security, or major changes in the overarching systems are discussed in this round. Pain points resulting from the coordination or those that already existed beforehand are resolved by the round and, if necessary, transferred to joint projects. The Council of Data Stewards repeatedly gives the company the opportunity to create a "we-feeling" among the employees entrusted with data challenges. Data challenges can only be solved as a team by all employees in the company working together. This spirit of cooperation and collaboration must exist decisively for overarching coordination to ensure long-term corporate success in the face of the multitude of challenges posed by digital transformation.

Round Table of Data Owners
In the annual Data Governance council, the Round Table of Data Owners, the progress of the Data Governance program is discussed with executives and top management. The aim is to align the strategic requirements of management and the existing expectations toward Data Governance, and at the same time to ensure that top management continues to support the Data Governance program by communicating its success. In some companies, an operational steering committee for the Data Governance program is added to the Round Table of Data Owners. A steering committee enables the Data Governance office and thus the Data Governance program to be controlled by top management in even shorter cycles. This can be particularly useful during the implementation phase in order to centralize and channel the high level of communication required with executives.

The structures and roles of Data Governance seem surprisingly complex to many at first. Particularly for small and medium-sized companies, there is a lot of organization here that apparently cannot be mapped 1:1. However, there are two things that need to be taken into account: First, complex challenges cannot be solved with a flip of a switch. Unfortunately. And second, this organizational structure presented here is an ideal, not a paradigm. It's important to understand that these structures are scalable and only appropriate in organizations where a variety of data challenges exist. Thus, Data Governance that is integrated into organizational units and mapped with structures and roles is primarily suitable for mid-sized companies and large corporations. Data Governance can only be effective in an environment characterized by complexity. In a company with only one corporate data space, there is no need for higher-level structures (Data Governance office, Council of Data Stewards, and Council of Data Owners) to ensure coordination. However, in a corporation with 150 or more corporate data spaces, meaningful management of data is no longer possible without these structures. Use the knowledge of data organization structures like a construction kit for your company. Take the elements that fit you and develop a customized data organization for your company. Leave out everything else that you don't need in your company. A good data organization works. A good data organization is as lean as possible. And a good data organization delivers direct value to your business. Additionally, keep in mind the separation of data organization building and directly solving data problems in data projects and your Data Governance will be successful.

In the second part, "Success Factors for Implementing Data Governance," we will again discuss in detail other important basics for successful Data Governance, before going into more depth on the data organization structure using clear process models in the subsequent third part.

References

DAMA International (2017) DAMA-DMBOK: data management body of knowledge, 2nd edn. Technics Publications, New Jersey

Ladley J (2012) Data governance: how to design, deploy and sustain an effective data governance program. Academic Press, Cambridge, Cambridge

Madsen L (2019) Disrupting data governance: a call to action. Technics Publications, New Jersey

Seiner R (2014) Non-invasive data governance: the path of least resistance and greatest success. Technics Publications, New Jersey

Soares S (2015a) The chief data officer handbook for data governance. MC Press, Boise

Soares S (2015b) Data governance tools: evaluation criteria, big data governance, and alignment with enterprise data management. MC Press, Boise

Templar M (2017) Get governed: building world class data governance programs. Ivory Lady Publishing, Wexford

Part II

Design

Success Factors for the Implementation

3

Abstract

A large number of Data Governance initiatives fail already in the implementation phase. The reasons for failure are manifold and often very individual. However, if we look at the other side and search for commonalities in Data Governance implementations that are sustainably successful, we can see clear success factors from which we can learn for the development of our own Data Governance. In this chapter, we branch out into the importance that resourcing, identifying issues and challenges as implementation drivers, and empowering staff in Data Management skills can have on the implementation success of Data Governance. We also delve into initial soft factors such as value-added principles, organizational structures, communications, and corporate culture. This chapter is intended as a good compass to prevent you from getting off the successful implementation path of a Data Governance rollout right at the beginning.

3.1 Provide Resources

While it is very easy for many companies to identify data problems as the cause and development barrier for lack of progress in the digital transformation, the same companies often find it very difficult to allocate resources to a functioning data organization that could solve the existing problems. There are many good reasons for this and, unfortunately, often many not so good reasons. Below are a few examples of common resource-blocking statements:

- There is a general lack of resources or the resources are just needed more urgently in other places.
- Data can also be maintained in parallel by other units.
- There is no data problem at all, but an IT problem.

© Springer-Verlag GmbH Germany, part of Springer Nature 2022   49
L. M. Bollweg, *Data Governance for Managers*, Management for Professionals,
https://doi.org/10.1007/978-3-662-65171-1_3

In essence, all these and similar reasons can always be traced back to the fact that corporate management sees data merely as an abstract accessory to the "really important things" and does not recognize and treat the data itself as a valuable asset ("data is an asset"). This is the only way to explain the fact that companies unhesitatingly allocate resources to the management of a vehicle fleet, but not to the professional management of data.

As a practitioner in Data Management, this passive attitude toward data is unfortunately still very common in the executive floors. This is largely due to the experience that successful managers have gained over the last few decades of their careers. Frequently, one encounters statements such as: "In the past, it was still possible without it." Unfortunately, these executives still haven't understood that for companies of all sizes and in all industries, the basis of competition has changed elementarily. Digital transformation has been swallowing up one traditional industry after another for decades, and no industry will be spared by the changes of the digitalization in the future. The transformation process may be slower in one industry or another, such as food retailing, or the transformation may not take hold until much later, as is currently the case in furniture retailing. However, wherever there is potential for automation that can be achieved through digitalization, this will undoubtedly be exploited sooner or later. The market for digital opportunities will take care of all this. The question is always: Does a company use its own digital potential independently, thus shaping the market itself and driving its competitors? Or do the existing competitors exploit the digital potential more quickly and drive ahead of them?

Whatever position a company finds itself in, driver or driven, first mover or first follower, the first impulse for change, the first impulse for digital transformation always starts with a company recognizing the value of digitalization. And it treats data as the fuel of digitalization in the same way it treats all its other valuable assets: professionally. And that means: Data must be managed as part of the digital infrastructure in order to serve the company's goals to the maximum.

> **Principle 15:** For successful implementation of Data Governance, management must recognize the value of data and allocate the necessary resources for its implementation.

Known misjudgments such as those mentioned above not only lead to uncontrollable and incalculable data problems, but often also to the fact that costly further development projects from the category of "Artificial Intelligence, Machine Learning, and Data Science" are initiated as a fig leaf for the digitalization ambitions of the company and fail again immediately (Plotkin 2013). It was simply missed to professionally evaluate and prepare their own data situation and quality. This pattern of high ambitions and painful failure, even with multiple attempts, especially for truly meaningful and value-added projects such as predictive analytics or automation, is already a classic today. These prestige projects are often started with a lot of management attention and only late in the course of the project it is realized that the required data does not represent the corresponding breadth of content (thematic scope of the information) or depth (necessary attributes). In other words, the data quality does not fit. Often, even the most elementary data keys for merging or joining the data are missing within the data, as well as the know-how to produce them subsequently. As a result, companies burn valuable budget and are surprised that only the large US companies seem to succeed in creating value with data.

However, the fact that the company has already made the decisive mistakes at the beginning of the chain (Create, Read, Update, Delete), in the creation and maintenance of its own data, is often only recognized by many companies due to external pressure or thanks to a long series of failed and costly projects.

This is precisely where modern Data Management and a meaningful Data Governance program come in. It is not enough to merely devote attention to Data Management. Data Governance must further develop data and the data capabilities of a company. For this task, Data Governance is the foundational tool of Data Management. Data Governance prepares a company's organizational and operational structure for existing and upcoming data-related challenges. And if you look around companies today, there are no more business challenges without data.

In addition, an exciting phenomenon can be observed in many traditional companies: when talking to managers and executives on a meta-level about the future and the challenges ahead, digital transformation and the value of data are always a clear priority. In practice, however, when it comes to concrete decisions about day-to-day work and the professional handling of data in the company, this realization still all too often falls victim to direct constraints or the lack of one's own skills. Dealing with data and implementing digitalization requires familiarization with often unfamiliar topics, even from executives. IT, data, and digitalization— these are all topics with barriers to entry. That's why Data Governance is still uncharted territory for many decision-makers and not clearly within their grasp. For this reason, it is understandable that considerable communication efforts are always to be expected when setting up Data Governance. This will be discussed in more detail later in section "3.6—Communicate Intensively and Involve Stakeholders."

Let's move away from the challenges and look forward. Data Governance initiatives today are generally afforded by two groups of companies. First, large enterprises that can provide the resources for professional Data Management. And second, companies for which data is a direct part of the value chain, for example, companies such as information service and digital service providers.

But if you think about the second group, the question arises which medium-sized company today does not belong to this group in one way or another. Today, data accompanies and controls virtually all value chains, from the production of raw materials to further processing and delivery of the products to the consumer. Not to mention marketing and sales.

Any information processing and exchange, within and between enterprise planning systems (ERP, PPS, etc.) and with suppliers' and customers' systems, relies on high data quality and optimal data processes to successfully serve its business purposes.

So in the end, it's the same as with any change and any change process: companies often only adapt their way of working when they can no longer achieve their goal and thus their success with the usual methods and procedures. Only when the pain is palpable and the pressure is high does the willingness to change begin. It is absurd and short-sighted, but it corresponds to reality. That is why it is important to demonstrate the urgency of change again and again. Data Governance is nothing else but change. And that is why the same rules apply to Data Governance: Data Governance always becomes interesting when a company encounters challenges that it can no longer solve without professional Data Management.

When this moment has been reached and awareness of the value of Data Governance has been recognized in the company, then the company will no longer find it difficult to provide the necessary resources. Without resources for the professional management of data, the company cannot expect any development. Data Governance without resources is a toothless tiger. It changes nothing in the company— everything would remain the same.

3.2   Identify Implementation Drivers

And it is precisely this realization that resources are needed that provides the first important starting point to consider when implementing Data Governance. You have to ask yourself the question: "How can you justify within the company that the required resources are made available? How can you show that implementing Data Governance is an undertaking that adds value and earns the trust of leadership?" A helpful tool for answering these questions is the identification of implementation drivers (Ladley 2012).

▶ An implementation driver is an issue that is understandable and familiar to everyone in the company (employees as well as managers), and which represents a problem that needs to be solved so urgently that the company shows willingness to change.

Ideally, the change is even requested as a service. Classic implementation drivers are data quality issues and legal regulations such as the GDPR. But they can also be other issues, such as competition or possible efficiency gains through automation. Of course, it can also be several drivers at the same time. What the right topics are to convince the company varies from company to company. Very often, however, the identified and communicated driver forms the basis for the subsequent success or failure of the implementation attempt of Data Governance. Only when the driver is understood by everyone in the company and the company is really prepared to develop its organization further to solve the problem, will the implementation of Data Governance be successful in the long term.

Principle 16: Before implementing Data Governance, at least one clear implementation driver must be identified. This should show the company in which areas Data Governance solves important business problems and thus generate a willingness to change.

In the course of implementation, you will perceive that the communicated driver changes from time to time. The company's view and goals change, and with it the prioritization of data challenges. The key here is to stay in touch with the management level and keep your finger on the pulse. It is important to think about these changing prioritizations of the management level in the design of the Data Governance program. In doing so, it makes sense to create a responsive organization. Not only at the data level, but also with regard to stakeholder management. Because the sustainable anchoring and further development of the data organization is the actual, major challenge. And this can only be mastered if top management support is also ensured in the long term.

3.3   Develop Data Management Capabilities

In addition to the structure of the data organization, the capabilities of the company in the implementation of Data Management practices are a decisive success factor. Before delving into what specific practices and methods a Data Management department needs to successfully operate Data Governance, it makes sense to delve into the importance of the strategic alignment of Data Management capabilities.

As for every function mapped in a company, it is also necessary for the control and development of Data Management capabilities to align them with corporate goals. In larger companies, the best way to translate business goals into concretely required capabilities is to develop a data strategy with a corresponding implementation plan. In smaller companies, the data strategy and implementation plan can also merge. A good data strategy serves as a compass for Data Management, Data Governance, and all employees involved to guide their own actions and further development. The detailed development of a data strategy, as important as it may be for the success of Data Governance, is not part of this book. Nevertheless, to reflect this fact and to do justice to the importance of strategic alignment, it is reiterated at this point that it is important for the success of Data Governance to discuss Data Management practices not only categorically but also with a strategic lens. For the planning of a Data Governance, the concrete practices of Data Management should not be considered as stand-alone functional building blocks, but their strategic importance for the required culture change must also be considered in the sense of an accompanying change management (DAMA International 2017). For example, implementing BI tools and using them to retrieve, analyze, and transform data, as well as create reports, is a key competency for modern Data Management. However, it is only when these tools are also made available to the business departments and a large number of employees independently create reports and analyses that this competence also has a beneficial effect on business transformation. The whole success of digital transformation follows the insight that it is not enough to put a new tool into the hands of a specialized employee and hope for the best for the company. It is also necessary to explain to the specialist that he, too, must train other employees in the use of the tool and what purpose the use and the technological development serve.

In order to sharpen this view, both strategic orientation points and concrete capabilities to which good Data Management, and thus good Data Governance, can be aligned will be explored in greater depth.

Proactive Instead of Reactive
One of the first most important culture changes is to get out of the reactive state of only responding to data problems as a fire department. The goal is to get into a proactive state, that is, to optimize problematic data before it causes pain in the company.

For everyday reality, it can be concluded that today in most companies Data Management still has only a reactive character. Data problems occur and cause business problems. These have to be solved at full speed. Data Management starts by working out the data problem and, after a few loops, usually solves it. After that, Data Management then lies down again and waits for the next problem.

This somewhat pointed and provocative description of the often strenuous work of employees in Data Management should not be broken down to the performance of individual employees. That would not do justice to the often passionate commitment of Data Management staff. Rather, it describes an organizational problem. Many Data Management departments are structurally organized and staffed in such a way that they are only able to have a reactive impact in the company. They are often too far removed from the business units and the problems of everyday work to be able to provide meaningful proactive impulses. As a result, many Data Management departments are left with only the role of firefighters. Only in the case of critical corporate problems do they come to the attention of top management; otherwise, they operate largely unnoticed in the shadows of the IT systems.

Companies in which Data Management is supposed to develop future-oriented data architectures for digital value creation from this sideline are bound to fail. These companies miss out on bringing Data Management into the role of the pacemaker, the developer of information structures, and profiting from the proactive development impulses that come off in the process.

But it is not just the organizational structure and the corporate environment that cannot be directly influenced. Data Management departments also often fail themselves in the development from "reactive" to "proactive." Proactive Data Management is, of course, always a strategic direction that an organization must take. But it is also a mindset that the employees in Data Management and the employees in Data Governance must develop themselves (see Fig. 3.1).

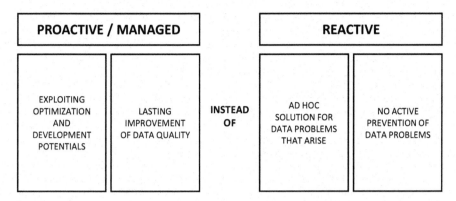

Fig. 3.1 Benefits of proactive data management © Lars Michael Bollweg 2022. All Rights Reserved

The importance of this second point cannot be overstated. When employees begin to establish the proactive mindset in their daily work, i.e., when they proactively deal with data quality and data processes in the company, they not only reduce the number of problematic data errors in the company, but they also permanently show the company potential for further digital development. In other words, they proactively accompany the company on the path to digital transformation.

For a company, proactive Data Management therefore means that it gets a clear view of itself through the number of optimization and development potentials found. Where does the company stand today? Where could it develop digitally in the future? And it is precisely the knowledge of the existing optimization potential that forms the basis for a continuous improvement dynamic, which changes to a real development perspective as the level of maturity increases. Proactive Data Management is like a first stone that sets a big slope in motion with a small push. The proactive minimum in Data Management is for entrepreneurs the often urgently needed impetus, for which an organization is only waiting inside to tackle and overcome the challenges of digitalization and digital transformation with creativity and innovation.

Unified Data Language
In order to intensify the development dynamics even further, a common language for dealing with data is an important foundation that many companies are establishing within a data strategy. In addition to the standardization of technical terms around data, a uniform understanding of the data organization and the data processes is one of the most important building blocks of a common data language. Expanding the view from dormant data within databases to organized data in data spaces and moving data in data processes along the company's processes is particularly helpful in everyday business. A company should explain this change of perspective to all its employees in simple words and ideally also with pictures, charts, and diagrams. See the following figure (Fig. 3.2) with an example for the distinction between data spaces and data processes:

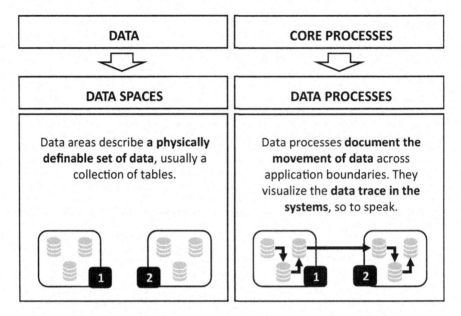

Fig. 3.2 New perspectives in data management—Data spaces and data processes © Lars Michael Bollweg 2022. All Rights Reserved

Principle 17: Data Management skills are more than just data skills. A proactive mindset and a common language are equally critical to success.

Data Management Practices

Data Management practices build on the frameworks introduced in the previous sections (Proactive Mindset and Unified Data Language). Data Management practices comprise procedures and methods for the professional handling of data within companies and organizations. The seven most important categories here are:

(a) Data project management
(b) Basics in IT infrastructure, system architecture, and business processes
(c) Data and data process documentation
(d) Data engineering (CRUD & ETL)
(e) Data analytics and BI
(f) Data requirements management
(g) Data quality management

Since this book is not a textbook for teaching these core competencies in Data Management, the individual categories are only briefly addressed and the most important aspects in each topic are highlighted. For more in-depth coverage of the core competencies, reference should be made to the large number of existing educational offerings which discuss these topics in detail and in the necessary depth. A perfect introduction to the breadth of Data Management capabilities is provided by the standard work of the Data Management Community—DAMA-DMBOK: Data Management Body of Knowledge (DAMA International 2017).

(a) Data Project Management The ability to manage projects independently is one of the key competencies for successful Data Management and thus one of the key competencies for operating Data Governance. The ability to identify data projects and prepare their importance for the company in a structured manner, for example using the Six Sigma approach DMAIC or similar process models, should be emphasized. Data projects always require some form of investment, time, and/or development costs. These expenses must be justified within the company and the decision-makers must be convinced of the benefits.

The ability to break down large, complex, and often process-related data projects into small, solvable subtasks is crucial to success. To bring order into the projects, Data Management is helped by representations along the CRUD data lifecycle. In particular, the focus on data creation and data usage as well as the representation of these within a data and system process representation enables data projects to be structured quickly and easily into concrete work packages. This form of operationalization enables data project managers to quickly achieve initial results and work through projects in a targeted manner.

The procedure is very simple and is performed in three steps: (1) start point/end point analysis, (2) data process documentation, and (3) task package identification.

(1) Start point/end point analysis: In order to develop and prepare a data challenge within project planning, a project team sensibly starts with a start point/end point analysis along the data process. This means starting by capturing the data creators (starting points—e.g., employees or systems) involved in the data process. In many cases, it makes sense to record the type of data creation (e.g., system-based, manual, semi-automated). This information is needed in the third step, the task package identification.

After all starting points of the data process are known, the data users are recorded. The data users are the controlling entity in the data process. The data users have this prominent position in the process because the data must serve their needs. That means the data must be fit for use. The data users therefore define the data requirements on the basis of which the required data quality is evaluated in the data process. A data user is therefore also referred to synonymously as a data requester. In a start point/end point analysis, one aims to capture all data requesters inside and outside the company. At this point, it is worth going into more detail: Recording the requirements of the data users is the key to assessing the data process quality and thus also the data quality ("fit to use"). Based on this, it makes sense to invest especially in the elicitation of data requirements. The assessment of data process and data quality is always only as good as the known requirements allow. For a particularly high level of maturity of Data Governance, it is therefore always necessary to intensify communication with data users in order to ideally align data

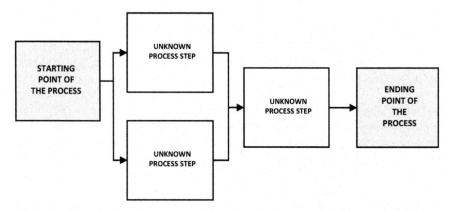

Fig. 3.3 Start point and end point analysis Step 1 © Lars Michael Bollweg 2022. All Rights Reserved

and data processes with their requirements. And, of course, it is also important to document the recorded data requirements in a structured manner (see Fig. 3.3).

(2) **Data process documentation:** After the start and end points as well as the type of data creation and the existing data requirements have been captured, it is important to document the complete data process in the systems, the so-called data lineage. A data process can also be described as a data trace in the systems. Documenting the data process answers the questions, "Where does the data come from? Where does it go? This documentation can be mapped using various systems (e.g., a data catalog or data modeling tool) or simply in a schematic drawing, e.g., in PowerPoint. The simple illustration is quite sufficient to complete a data project planning. Of course, the accompanying documentation in an appropriate software often develops advantages or synergy effects for subsequent further projects and is generally considered as the professional documentation space. Nevertheless, it is not necessary to wait for the introduction of these complex software solutions if you can directly create an overview and structure with simple means (see Fig. 3.4).

(3) **Task package identification:** With the results from the first two steps (start point/end point analysis and data process documentation), one now has all the information at hand to transform each complex data challenge into individual task packages. Another time the concept of complexity reduction comes into play. To identify necessary measures and to optimize the data process, one uses the known data requirements as an evaluation criterion for each station arising in the data process. A station can be the data situation in a system: Does the data in the system match the requirements? No—Then data cleansing may be necessary. And this creates a first task package. Does the data transformation in the interfaces match the requirements? No—Then further development of the interface may be necessary. And another task package is identified. Does the data generation fit the requirements? No—Then input validation may be necessary. And it is no surprise now: another task package is tailored. Once the individual task packages

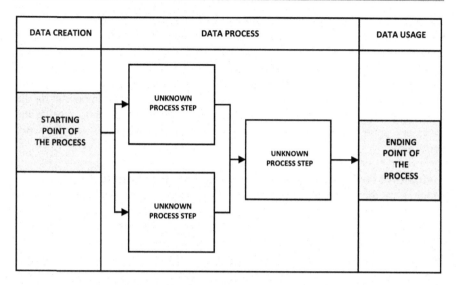

Fig. 3.4 Start point and end point analysis Step 2 © Lars Michael Bollweg 2022. All Rights Reserved

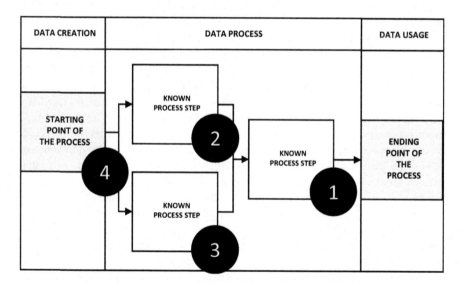

Fig. 3.5 Identification of task packages © Lars Michael Bollweg 2022. All Rights Reserved

have been identified, the project plan for working through the data project has virtually come into being by itself (see Fig. 3.5).

This briefly outlined procedure is just one example of many of how complex corporate and data processes can be easily and professionally transferred into solvable task packages and the processing can be started in a targeted manner. However, creating a project plan and implementing it is not all that is necessary for successful project management. For the conclusion of projects it is still of great importance that the communication about the project conclusion and the changes connected with it reaches also all participants in the enterprise. Far too often, great efforts are made in Data Management to bring complex projects to a successful conclusion, but only a few people in the company are informed about it. A successful data project therefore always ends with a final presentation. This is important for the client, but also for the employees in Data Management, in order to receive the necessary appreciation in the company and from the executives for the work performed.

(b) Basics of IT Infrastructure, System Architecture, and Business Processes In addition to the technical competencies for handling data, Data Management employees need basic knowledge of all the disciplines with which Data Management works hand in hand in the company and also of all the topics with which they regularly come into contact. In addition to the many subject-specific topics that vary from company to company, however, the topics (1) IT infrastructure, (2) system architecture, and (3) enterprise processes are particularly worthy of mention here.

IT infrastructure: Data Management operates at the nexus of IT systems, and the employees involved therefore need a basic understanding of IT infrastructures. The IT infrastructure includes all layers that are required for the operation of an application or an IT system. The IT infrastructure therefore includes both hardware and software components. In simplified terms, three levels are often assumed. The hardware level, where you find physical servers and computers, the operating system level, where the foundation for the IT system that will later run is created, and finally the software level, where the actual application runs. Of course, this simplified view does not do justice to the complex reality. For a data manager, however, it holds a clear access point to the required knowledge. At the hardware level, the most important components and parts should be known (e.g., server, OnPrem vs. cloud, router, enterprise service bus). At the operating system level, the fundamental differences between Linux-based operating systems and Windows operating systems should be known (e.g., open source vs. closed source). And there should also be a basic understanding of how to handle and implement software.

In addition to the three levels of IT infrastructure, a special focus topic for the data manager in this context is of course the understanding of databases (SQL, NoSQL, GraphDB, etc.). Databases are the natural habitat of structured data and form the basis of data work in the company.

System architecture: Once a basic understanding of the individual components of the IT infrastructure has been gathered, it makes sense to deepen this further by looking at the system or IT architecture. The system architecture comprises the construction and connection plan of the individual applications and the IT systems on the IT infrastructure. The system architecture thus answers the question of which systems are present in the company and how they are interconnected, e.g., via data interfaces. However, the system architecture usually goes one step further. It not only depicts the actual status of the systems, but also shows the upcoming and future changes to the landscape. It is precisely this view of the changes that repeatedly assumes great importance for Data Management, which must provide support particularly frequently in the case of migrations and interface issues.

Business processes: Having acquired a basic understanding of IT infrastructure and system architecture, it is important to understand that the two structure-giving areas presented are not developed in a vacuum. IT, i.e., information technology with all its facets (IT infrastructure, system architecture, and, yes, data architecture as well), serves to fulfill enterprise processes. Without the connection of IT to the business processes, a meaningful assessment about the deployment quality of data, data in systems, the systems alone, the systems on the infrastructure, and the infrastructure itself is not possible. A data manager must therefore also see this connection and internalize the work in and on the processes as the very own work of Data Management.

Of course, the data manager does not have to become a professional process manager, but he must be familiar with a few basic concepts. A classic business process maps a value creation process in the company, which usually concludes with the handover to an internal or external customer. This customer orientation is equally important for the process and the data process in order to generate a quality statement about the service provided. A well-designed process is preferably delivered "End to End/E2E," i.e., from end to end or even beginning to end of the process chain. "E2E" means that the process maps all activities involved in the company (upstream as well as downstream), i.e., really all activities required for process fulfillment.

Particularly in large companies, there is a certain tendency to define processes within departments and areas of responsibility and to orient the process consideration to the boundaries of responsibility, the departmental boundaries. As a result, important interfaces and possible new and changing customer requirements often remain invisible to upstream and downstream process actors. An E2E view overcomes these blind spots and is a necessary basis for successful process work.

In addition, for many employees who are not actively involved in process development and documentation, it is helpful to understand how great the degree of design freedom and thus the degree of variance within a process design can be. While the process goal or even the topic of the process is often clear (production of individual parts, delivery of online orders, etc.), the consideration of the individual activities in the process is a matter of philosophy and focus. Quite similar to the "description of reality" in the creation of data, the documentation of a company process is also subject to a selection and choice process. In addition to different levels (e.g., ACTUAL, IDEAL, TARGET), the different granularity of the process documentation (all physical activities are documented/only the most important activities are documented) should also be mentioned here. Due to the closeness of the design activities of both disciplines (data architecture design and process design), a data manager quickly finds himself on familiar terrain in process work. It is precisely the insights into the design scope available to a large extent in enterprise process design, i.e., the triad of data, systems, and the activities in the processes, that take Data Management to a new evolutionary level. The triad of data, systems, and processes is often also referred to as business architecture and forms another key competence for efficient and goal-oriented further development of companies. The design and utilization of a business architecture will be discussed in greater detail in the following chapters.

(c) Data and Data Process Documentation The lack of knowledge about data in systems and data processes via interfaces is one of the biggest barriers to the further development of companies in the context of digital transformation.

Therefore, one of the most important tasks within Data Management is to establish a culture of data and data process documentation within the company. For this purpose, it is necessary to enable employees to prepare such documentation in a goal-oriented manner.

Data documentation: When documenting data, there are two perspectives that make up good data documentation. One is the documentation of data structures, which shows what data exists and in what form this data is expressed (what and where). Data structures documentation is therefore documentation along systems and resources (e.g., databases), data tables, and data columns. This documentation creates a clear view of the data stock in the company and enables searching and finding as well as the management of the known data stock.

In addition to the documentation of structures, a documentation of the data meaning, the so-called data definitions, is another mainstay of data documentation. While the structural documentation thus enables quantitative statements about data, the data definition creates a qualitative statement about the meaning of the data. An example of a good but comprehensive data definition can be found in the appendix of the book.

Data process documentation: The documentation of data processes has already been presented in the section on data project management and is therefore only repeated here for the sake of completeness. A look at common data problems in companies shows that the cause of most problems cannot be explained and resolved with a pure "point view" within a database. Often, data is part of complex processes and moves from one system to another within a data lifecycle. Data process documentation aims to represent these data movements between systems in a transparent and traceable manner. However, documenting the data process, or data lineage, is not a trivial matter. For one thing, it is costly to research data processes between and within systems because they are not visible from the outside. On the other hand, complex maps and graphs with many connecting lines (uni- and bidirectional) are created, which are difficult to depict with common graphics and presentation tools.

Once these challenges have been overcome, the documentation of data processes provides a valuable store of knowledge that is helpful for business and IT departments alike. Such documentation makes it easier for business departments to understand information flows and to push for changes and further developments. And for IT, this information forms direct handouts for implementing the required developments and saves developers a great deal of effort in "reengineering" the data flows within and between systems.

Helpful tools for process simplification and support in the daily implementation of simple data documentation and more complex data process documentation can be data catalogs, interface documentation software, and data modeling software.

(d) Data Engineering (CRUD and ETL)   It goes without saying that data handling is one of the most important core competencies within a Data Management department. As with data documentation, data handling also takes place along the dimensions described in the previous section of point consideration (within databases) and process consideration (between databases).

In the context of data that is viewed selectively, we often also speak of dormant data. This dormant data is classically processed within databases, systems, and evaluations along the CRUD perspective (Create, Read, Update, Delete) and forms the fuel for digitalization.

The data processing of process-related or dynamic data is similar, but quite different. Data that is in motion is usually passed along the ETL perspective (Extract, Transform, Load) via interfaces within the system landscape from one system to the other. Since this dynamic data can only in a few cases also be processed within the target systems in the same form as in the source system, it is prepared for the destination while still in transit. The data is fetched from the source database (Extract), prepared for use in the target system (Transform), and then stored in the target system (Load).

Useful skills for successful data engineering include knowledge of database languages such as SQL, NoSQL, and common database exchange formats such as CSV, XML, JSON, and others. Of course, an in-depth discussion of these points cannot be provided in a book like this, but it is important to understand that these skills are critical to the success of Data Management. The more employees are able to develop data within and between databases, the more powerful Data Management as a whole will be.

(e) Data Analytics and BI   In addition to the handling of data, the content-related evaluation and visual preparation of data is also part of the core skills of Data Management. Even though these two activities are often implemented together, e.g., in reporting and dashboards, they are based on fundamentally different competencies. Accordingly, the content analysis of data is also a discipline in its own right. Within this discipline, information that is available in data or data tables is usually evaluated and exploited with the help of statistical methods, e.g., descriptive or prescriptive statistics. This means that in evaluating the content of the data, knowledge is extracted from this information and then processed as a decision-making aid for other disciplines. This knowledge can then be found in statistical evaluations, reports, and key figures. As a rule, programming languages with a focus on data processing are used for the content analysis of data, such as Python, Scala, or R. As a bridging technology for employees without knowledge of programming languages, software solutions such as Rapid Minor or Knime are also often used, with which all data analyses and data transformations can be carried out within a graphical user interface.

The visual preparation of the data evaluated in terms of content, on the other hand, no longer takes place within the framework of the programming languages mentioned, even if these offer extensive libraries for this purpose. For the visualization of data, separate system worlds have developed along BI tools, e.g., Tableau and PowerBI, which are also open to employees without programming knowledge due to their simplicity in operation. In addition, these tools usually have simple functions with which the created visualizations can be easily shared within the company, e.g., via email or published, e.g., on dashboards.

While both statistical fundamentals and specialist knowledge form the working basis for the content-related evaluation of data, a basic understanding of visual communication is required above all for the visual preparation. The preparation of data within diagrams, charts, and graphics requires an intensive examination of the content, the target group, and the intended message. A good statistician is not necessarily good at visualizing data on dashboards.

(f) Data Requirements Management The importance of data requirements for the professional management of data has already been emphasized several times in the previous sections. Of course, the collection and documentation of data requirements is also a subcategory of Data Management to be considered separately—data requirements management.

Data requirements management is the structured confrontation of Data Management with the data requirements of a company's specialist departments. Or in other words, data requirements management is the answer to the question: What should or must data do? What business purposes does data serve? What will data be needed for in the future?

Very few companies today already deal with data requirements in a structured and systematic way. As a rule of thumb, data requirements are only recorded selectively along pain points or development projects. Yet, it is precisely in the discussion and creation of transparency regarding data requirements where the great potential for a company lies. Only if the existing data requirements are known and the company responds to known and new requirements in a structured manner, then the company is really in a position to professionalize its handling of data, to optimize its data situations, and, ideally, even to use them to open up new business areas.

The challenge in documenting data requirements lies in the level of detail, the so-called granularity. How precisely must a data requirement be described so that a company can continue to work with it in a meaningful and targeted manner? Experience shows that the documentation of a data requirement meets professional standards as soon as it can be validated. This means that a data requirement must be translatable into a validation rule that can be run as a test against a data set. For example, the requirement for a data record that all rows in the "ZIP Code" column must be "100% filled" is a validatable data requirement. Simply stating that the department needs "addresses" is not sufficient for professional management of data. However, validation rules are deepened again in the course of data quality management.

Fig. 3.6 The four
perspectives of data
governance © Lars Michael
Bollweg 2022. All Rights
Reserved

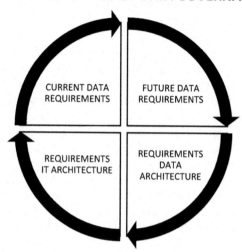

THE 4 PERSPECTIVES OF DATA GOVERNANCE

It can be valuable for companies to broaden their view when dealing with data requirements. It is not only interesting to capture the short-term, current, and immediate data requirements. The future, medium-term data requirements in a span of the next 3–5 years should also be made known as early as possible within the data organization. Only then will there be sufficient lead time to adjust data architectures and prepare data quality to meet future requirements. Of course, this assumes that the organization is looking to the future and strategically evolving its data and systems. Data Governance can be a useful driver and suitable forum for this debate.

(g) Data Quality Management Data quality management is the supreme discipline in Data Management because it requires and builds on all the previously mentioned capabilities to solve its challenges (Maydanchik 2012) (see Fig. 3.6). Meaningful data quality management always builds on professional project management that prioritizes incoming data problems along data requirements, evaluates them, and transfers them into work packages using a structured data quality process. To solve data problems, skills from both data engineering and data analytics are applied. The circle closes here. However, it still makes sense to go into the handling and approach to data quality problems a bit more in depth. To do this, we will first look at the basics of data quality management and then go through all the content discussed up to this point again along a classic data quality process.

Fundamentals of Data Quality Management
The most important basis for data quality management is always the answer to the question: What actually is data quality?

▶ Data quality, as defined in this book, is the result of validating known data requirements against existing data. Data quality is the measurement of whether data is fit to use or not.

The first part of the definition, validation of "known data requirements," is important because validation against unknown requirements is impossible. The assessment of a data quality is always only as good as the known data requirements allow. Without a clear, unambiguous, and validatable definition of what the data requirements are, no data quality assessment can be produced.

To measure data quality, data requirements are translated into validation rules. These validation rules enable a quality check, i.e., a validation of the data. When validating the data, each row of one or more columns runs against the validation rules and returns a truth value. The row matches the validation rule: "1" or "True." Or the row does not match the validation rule: "0" or "False." The number of respective return values can be used to statistically represent the quality assessment with the help of the data quality score.

Principle 18: Data quality can only be measured if the data requirements have been captured beforehand and validated against the data. Knowledge about data requirements is just as valuable to a company as knowledge about the data itself.

A value of 100% means that 100% of the data fits the known data requirements. A value of 75% means that only 75% of the data fits the known data requirements. The important thing to understand here is that a data quality score can only be as good as the data requirements that an organization knows. This is why the data requirements management capability is such a critical one. If an organization is poor at gathering its own data requirements and translating them into validation rules, then that organization's data quality management will not be successful either (see Fig. 3.7).

Even though this book only touches on the topic of data quality and the focus is on the topic of Data Governance, it should be added for the sake of completeness that a 100% data quality assessment in itself is not a meaningful development goal for a company. It is better to focus on an ever dynamic positive development of the data quality assessment while at the same time permanently increasing the number of known data requirements for the data set. Only if the data requirements are constantly increasing, i.e., the company is successively adding more and more value with the data and therefore the development around the data is dynamic, then the company is on the right track. Of course, a stagnant number of data requirements fulfilled over a long period of time is not bad per se. But it does indicate that development is no longer taking place in the system and the area in which the data quality is collected. And this is always an indicator of missed opportunities and unused potential for further development (see Fig. 3.8).

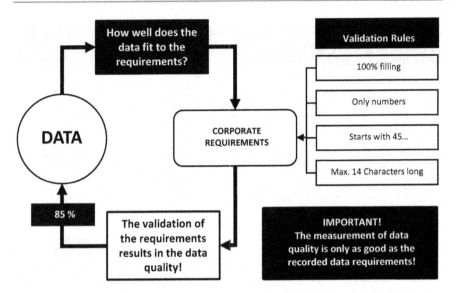

Fig. 3.7 What is data quality? © Lars Michael Bollweg 2022. All Rights Reserved

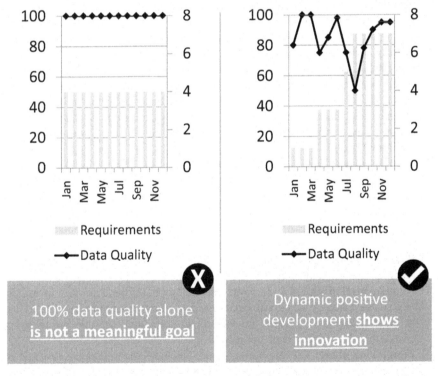

Fig. 3.8 The dynamic development of data quality © Lars Michael Bollweg 2022. All Rights Reserved

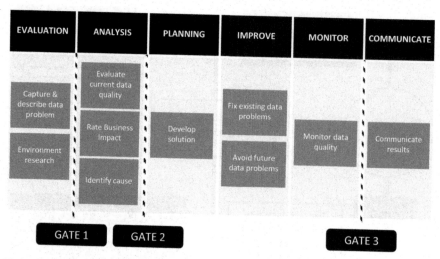

Fig. 3.9 Data quality management process © Lars Michael Bollweg 2022. All Rights Reserved

To ensure professional data quality management, a structured data quality management process can be helpful. A classic data quality process consists of six phases: (1) evaluation phase, (2) analysis phase, (3) planning phase, (4) implementation phase, (5) monitoring phase, and (6) communication and documentation phase (McGilvray 2008) (see Fig. 3.9).

(1) **Evaluation phase:** In the evaluation phase, the data problem is recorded superficially and its basic features are described. In addition, initial information about the environment (stakeholders, IT systems, company processes) is obtained and the context of the data problem is evaluated. At the end of the phase, a decision is made whether or not to set up a data project to solve the problem (Gate 1).

(2) **Analysis phase:** Only in the second phase more time and energy is invested in the deeper analysis of the problem. The current data situation is evaluated (quantitatively and qualitatively), the cause of the problem is identified, and the impact on the company is assessed. At the end of the second phase, it is again evaluated whether or not the data project will move into implementation (Gate 2).

(3) **Planning phase:** In the third phase, the actual solution to the problem is planned. The implementation of the necessary measures is thus prepared.

(4) **Implementation phase:** In the implementation phase, the necessary measures (e.g., data cleansing, data transformations, data coupling) are implemented. That is, the existing data problems are solved and additional measures are taken to ensure that the problem does not recur.

(5) **Monitoring phase**: The monitoring phase concludes the implementation and is optional. If the data is particularly sensitive and has a high impact on the company, or if the solution to the data problem does not allow the problem to be secured in the long term without a residual risk, technical monitoring of the data (data monitoring) may be appropriate. At the end of the monitoring phase, a

decision is made together with the client as to whether the project should be completed.

(6) **Communication and documentation phase:** And of course it is purposeful to present and document the results at the end of data quality projects. On the one hand, this has the purpose of informing the client and the company about the completion of the project; on the other hand, it is also an important communication point for the transfer of knowledge into Data Management and the entire company.

Unfortunately, it is not uncommon for well-intentioned further developments of data layers to develop a life of their own over time due to a lack of information and communication with employees, for example because of new data quality problems, and thus to become a problem themselves. This can be avoided through good project documentation and communication.

Only when Data Management has developed the skills listed here as examples for the professional handling of data in the company, or is at least in the process of developing these skills, does it make sense to take the next steps toward implementing Data Governance. Without these skills, Data Governance would be a toothless tiger that would be able to point out data problems, but would have no chance of making a constructive contribution.

3.4   Select the Organizational Structure

Once you have identified the driver(s) for implementation within the enterprise and convinced senior management to implement Data Governance, the next challenge is to design the organizational and scaling model of the data organization with which you want to realize the implementation. The organizational model shows what the end picture of Data Governance should look like within a company. In other words, it is the blueprint or outline for Data Governance. The scaling model shows the way in which one would like to achieve the organizational model, i.e., with which procedure and in which steps one would like to establish the organizational model as a whole in the company (Gascoigne 2019) (see Fig. 3.10).

For both of the required models (organization and scaling), two alternative approaches have emerged in each case as possible poles for orientation. These can either be implemented in pure form or one can use them as inspiration for a possible hybrid solution. (1) The Organization Model (Centralized/Federated/Hybrid Solutions) and (2) the Scaling Model (Use Case to Scale/Responsive Organization).

Principle 19: The successful implementation of Data Governance is based on a suitable organizational model and a suitable scaling model.

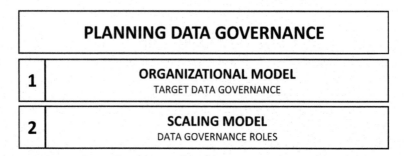

Fig. 3.10 Planning data governance © Lars Michael Bollweg 2022. All Rights Reserved

(1) The Right Organizational Model
Addressing the right organizational model is one of the most fundamental in implementing Data Governance. Over time, two organizational models for Data Governance programs have established themselves as the standard: the centralized model and the federal model.

The centralized model can also be referred to as the traditional approach. The model involves the introduction of a central Data Management unit within a company. This central unit is given the task of supporting the business units in managing the data. Data Governance provides this support as a service unit or service provider to the internal customer on demand. Of course, this has the charm that such a unit can be implemented within the company without much resistance. Unfortunately, however, this approach often fails because this central service offering generates too little added value for the company to justify the investment (return on investment). Why is this? Data problems and data challenges arise in a decentralized manner in modern companies. This means that all departments and areas generate, use, maintain, and delete data consistently and independently. All areas are under pressure to develop and optimize—the data situation develops dynamically. A central unit alone is not in a position to be everywhere in the company with all its employees, to know all the issues, and to transfer this collection of decentralized challenges into central solutions in a coordinated manner. In addition, it can often be observed that central units are disproportionately utilized by certain departments and areas of the company, while other areas in the company are not served at all. This is understandable. After all, central units often react most intensively to the most powerful or loudest requester and rest a bit with the less powerful or restrained requesters. The whole development of the company suffers as a result and becomes unbalanced. Individual areas are oversupplied, while others have not even received the basic digital support.

One can only blame the management of a central unit to a limited extent. Without an overall view of the existing data challenges, it is impossible for the department to prioritize the upcoming data projects in terms of their relevance. Since this problem of unevenly distributed forces has arisen in many companies in recent decades, the federative model was developed as a solution approach.

The federative model takes a modern approach compared to the centralized model. It follows the conviction that data problems arising in a decentralized manner and data challenges cannot be solved sustainably with a central Data Management unit alone. The federative model therefore proposes a culture change in the way data is handled and the importance of data to business success. It recommends that Data Management and the business units grow together as a team and that both sides work together, decentralized at the place where the data challenges arise, also on their solution. Data Management in the federative model is not offered to the business units as an external service, but is provided jointly by Data Management and the business units in the sense of co-creation. This means that Data Management sends employees to the departmental and process organization, and these employees work together with the departmental managers to drive forward the further development of data handling. This approach has proven to be the most effective because, in addition to the direct proximity to the specialist departments and the associated rapid resolution of existing pain points, it also achieves a multiplier effect in the other specialist departments. Through the joint collaboration of the specialist department and Data Management, the practices of professional Data Management are also established among the employees of the specialist department and the further development of the corporate culture is stimulated.

Hybrid solutions: Hybrid solutions should always be treated with caution. In general, they are only recommendable in very few exceptions. However, hybrid solutions often have the charm of helping to overcome political barriers in the implementation process. We speak of hybrid solution when Data Management is a supporting external service provider in one area of the business and grows into the organizational teams in other areas. Hybrid solutions enable this form of flexibility. If individual managers want to take a special path for their areas, hybrid solutions and combination options quickly provide a portfolio from which to draw. The danger, however, is that the cooperation capabilities of the individual areas will suffer as a result of hybrid solutions, and the advantage of reducing complexity through a uniform organization described in the first chapters will be lost again. Here, it is imperative to weigh up which focus is more valuable for the company: rapid implementation or a high degree of effectiveness of the data organization. When setting up a data organization, it is advisable to proceed as standardized as possible and to allow as few exceptions as possible. One solution to serve political constraints and establish standards at the same time is to find a hybrid approach to the standard, for example to only establish an exception for a period of time. This gives Data Governance the opportunity to build a relationship of trust with stakeholders and prove that the planned standardized approach is successful. Of course, this also comes with some risk; exceptions can become the standard over time. However, such an approach is at least better than accepting the exceptions as the standard from the start.

(2) The Right Scaling Model
The selection of the right scaling model is also a very decisive question when implementing Data Governance. As with the organizational models, two standards have become established here that can be used very well as a starting point for your

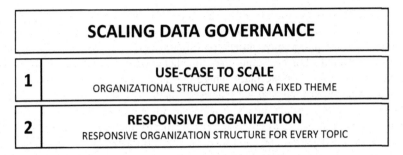

Fig. 3.11 Data Governance scaling models © Lars Michael Bollweg 2022. All Rights Reserved

own planning. The "Use Case to Scale" approach and the development of a "Responsive Organization" (see Fig. 3.11).

In the development of Data Governance, the **"Use Case to Scale"** approach is the classic approach that has certainly been used most frequently in recent years. This approach proposes the introduction of Data Governance via a concrete use case, for example, the introduction of Data Governance for deleting personal data. That is, along this use case, that the company's data capabilities are developed and Data Governance is introduced either centralized or federated. Very often, by the way, the "Use Case to Scale" approach is chosen together with the centralized organizational model. This is a good fit because both approaches aim to require as little change as possible in the enterprise, i.e., to keep effort and change to a minimum in order to encounter as little implementation resistance as possible. The "Use Case to Scale" approach pursues the goal of following up the introduction of the first successful use case with further use cases—i.e., to scale up in order to serve all known "use cases" in the company in the final expansion stage. This approach is said to have very good sustainability during implementation.

The strength of this approach—proceeding use case by use case—is at the same time its weakness. Building and developing the organization around a use case takes time and ties up resources in the company. During this time, however, the company will still encounter other topics and use cases that also need to be addressed. Due to the "use case approach," however, the data organization is very narrowly focused on one topic and the attention in the specialist departments is also very limited. This usually leads to other pain points and other potentials not being worked on and developed with the necessary intensity. In addition, when the next use case is implemented, the organization has to be expanded again, so the effort lies a second time in building up the organization with all its challenges, and thus a lot of time and focus is needed again. And this spiral of effort continues with each additional use case.

The **"Responsive Organization"** approach is a further development of the "Use Case to Scale" approach. This approach proposes a unique organizational structure that is directly capable of serving all use cases, i.e., all data challenges. The idea, then, is to save time during implementation and become capable of acting more quickly. This approach is necessarily dependent on a federated organization, as it would not be possible to map it centrally and without direct departmental involvement. The "Responsive Organization" requires all data trades (data project managers, data analysts, data engineers) within all departments of the organization to be able to react flexibly to different data challenges. The speed advantage of this approach comes from the fact that it actually turns the approach in the use case-driven approach upside down (flip-the-script). Whereas in the use case-driven approach, the problematic data is usually first sifted, mapped, and documented and then, starting from the problem, the organization is made capable of acting around this issue, in the case of scaling via a "Responsive Organization" one proceeds the other way around and first builds up the organization with experts and then defines it in detail. This approach works just as well in practice because the data experts from the specialist departments involved in the adaptive organization usually already have the required data knowledge and are therefore able to act immediately. So in the responsive organization, you first create structures, and only then do you start sifting through the individual data, mapping it, and documenting it. This is the authors' favored approach. However, there are also very good reasons that speak against this approach, for example, the high commitment that this approach requires in management. But, implemented correctly, this approach leads companies most quickly and effectively to the goal of an actionable data organization in the company.

With the "Responsive Organization," the strength is again the greatest weakness. Due to the intensive and extensive organizational setup without concrete commitment to defined "use cases," it is much more important for the "Responsive Organization approach" to clearly communicate its added value through data projects in the company. If this is not achieved, the implementation as a whole is quickly jeopardized, and the risk of burning a company out on the topic of Data Governance and making it difficult to start up again later is high.

3.5   Create Added Value: Right Away

For all organization and scaling models, it is important to directly achieve added value to justify the investment a company makes in the data organization. This is easier to communicate when an implementation proceeds along clearly communicated use cases. And it is more difficult at first glance if the implementation has to transform the organization and the culture in parallel, analogous to the "Responsive Organization" approach.

However, to overcome this problem equally for all approaches, it is first important to be aware of this challenge. The implementation of Data Governance is only justified if the implemented Data Governance supports the company in achieving business goals. As a rule, these are goals from the following three categories:

- Increase yields
- Reduce expenses
- Manage risks

Data Management can make valuable contributions in all three categories. These should be incorporated into the procedure parallel to the introduction of Data Governance. A sensible way to clearly communicate the added value of professional Data Management to internal stakeholders is to separate the implementation of Data Governance from the use cases that are implemented within data projects (Templar 2017).

Principle 20: To sustain top-level support, Data Governance must generate measurable added value for the company from the outset and communicate this.

It therefore makes sense to communicate Data Governance and its implementation as a single building block and to demonstrate the resulting added value within data projects separately, but ideally in parallel, to the stakeholders. This has a number of advantages. On the one hand, one is in a position to demonstrate the advantages of professional Data Management already at the beginning of the organizational setup in small data projects and to justify the changes that Data Governance forces in the company. On the other hand, the separation of organizational setup and data projects is useful and helpful. In the event that a data project is not successful, there is no direct link to the organizational structure. In this way, one secures the support for the organizational setup and, in the event of problems, burns much less earth (or motivated employees) than in the case of joint communication.

3.6   Communicate Intensively and Involve Stakeholders

The term "communication" has already been mentioned several times in the previous chapters. The importance of communication (status and success communication) is a very decisive factor during the implementation and further regular operation of Data Governance. Make sure that you keep the decision-makers permanently informed about the status of the implementation of Data Governance, involve them, and keep them very intensively involved in upcoming changes. Various formats are suitable for this purpose:

- Divisional and corporate presentations
- Steering committees
- Control dates
- 1:1—Meetings
- Rule Reporting
- Info mails/Newsletter
- Sounding Groups

As content for the communication, you should always have the story around your motive, i.e., your introduction driver, ready. "Why is Data Governance being introduced?" is a very decisive message that you should send over and over again. Ideally, this "why" will be further customized to each stakeholder group as the implementation progresses. Examples of area-related challenges should supplement the "why" in the course of the implementation and thus strengthen the personal concern of the stakeholders to be included.

Once the "why" has been included in the communication, it must be possible to communicate the vision, the target image of Data Governance, in clear and simple terms. Here, it is important to choose a narrative form that even non-data-savvy employees and managers can follow. Metaphors are a good way to make even very technical issues accessible to an audience that is not familiar with the subject.

Developing an overarching data strategy that identifies Data Governance as a building block and foundation of higher-level data measures can be helpful (Seiner 2014).

All communication efforts basically serve one purpose, to ensure ongoing top-level support for the implementation. This support is ensured by communicating the added value for the organization. Therefore, this communication should always be a success communication in addition to a pain point/problem communication. In other words, it must be regularly shown to all stakeholders in the company in which problems and projects Data Governance helps the company and why the investment in the program is therefore justified.

3.7   Data-Centric Corporate Culture

The introduction of Data Governance is not a purely technical development of the skills of a company's employees, but a deep intervention in the corporate culture. It is not only the procedures and methods of individual employees that are changed by Data Governance, but also the evaluation and utilization of existing information assets throughout the company. Therefore, it is of great importance to recognize that any introduction of Data Governance must also have a change management component in order to be successful. This means that the company must not only deal with the management of data in technical terms, but also with how all the people involved are to implement and realize these changes. In other words, how the employees can also accept this change, help shape it, and then implement it in their day-to-day work. The introduction of Data Governance is always about how the upcoming change can also become part of the corporate culture in order to have a lasting positive effect.

> **Principle 21:** Data Governance promotes a data-centric corporate culture and benefits from it at the same time. Data Governance is therefore also always change management and development of the corporate culture.

Fig. 3.12 The three dimensions of a corporate culture in data-driven companies © Lars Michael Bollweg 2022. All Rights Reserved

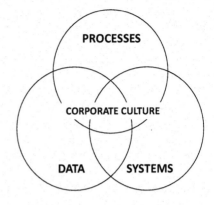

LEVELS OF CORPORATE CULTURE

1	**VISIBLE ARTIFACTS** WORK RESULTS / PRODUCTS
2	**FORMULATED VALUES** CORPORATE STRATEGY / CORPORATE VALUES
3	**BASIC PREMISES AND ASSUMPTIONS** BASIS OF ACTION OF THE EMPLOYEES

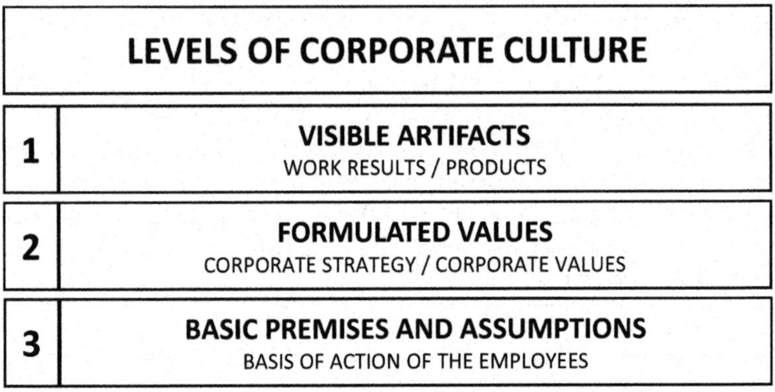

Fig. 3.13 Levels of corporate culture © Lars Michael Bollweg 2022. All Rights Reserved

The culture in a company or organization is formed by how employees and managers deal with the processes as well as the information, data, IT systems, and technologies of a company. In each of these categories (processes, data, systems), culture is expressed in different ways at different levels (see Fig. 3.12). In theory, there are roughly three levels (Schein and Schein 2018): (1) Visible artifacts, (2) formulated values, and (3) basic premises and assumptions (see Fig. 3.13).

At the top level, one finds the artifacts and visible structures such as the existing processes, the current handling of data, and the existing IT landscape. All these ACTUAL states are the result of an existing corporate culture and as such must not be negated. Below this visible level of artifacts lies the second level of formulated values. The level of formulated values comprises all values that have been recorded by the company, e.g., in corporate strategies and target images, and to which the company would like to orient itself in everyday work. It is only at the lowest level that one encounters the lived corporate culture. At a deeper level, a corporate culture is based on basic premises and assumptions of the employees with regard to working together. These basic premises can deviate greatly from the formulated values of a company if they are not lived and enforced by managers in everyday life.

A classic instrument for achieving cultural change at all levels in the company, resolving contradictions, and involving all employees at all levels (artifacts, formulated values, assumptions, and basic premises) is to include a cultural implementation (in this case of Data Governance) in addition to a technical one. The cultural implementation includes meetings and workshops with employees on how to deal with the upcoming challenges and changes and can be supported by joint implementation planning and firmly defined target agreements.

Accompanying the introduction of Data Governance, the impetus for further development in the direction of a "data-centric corporate culture" can make a valuable contribution to successfully mastering the upcoming change process as part of the digital transformation. For the design of a data-centric corporate culture, the creation of a set of values, e.g., a data manifesto within a data strategy, has become established, for example, to define the framework of cultural change. See the following examples:

- Data is an asset.
- Data is self-describing and requires no application or system for its interpretation and meaning.
- Data is created in open, non-proprietary formats.
- Data is made available to everyone in the company via documented interfaces and open APIs.
- Responsibility for access to data is the responsibility of data stewards and is not managed or controlled by IT.
- and many more...

The goal of introducing a data-centric corporate culture is for the company to change its view of data and treat data like its most important other economic goods (assets)—in other words, to manage it professionally. The introduction of a data-centric corporate culture should be seen as a cultural addition, not a cultural adoption. Other values of a corporate culture (such as innovation-driven, social, highly specialized, speed to market, cost efficiency, employee satisfaction and empowerment, fail fast and cheap) are not constrained by a data-centric corporate culture, but complemented. If there have been components of the corporate culture in the past that contradict a data-centric culture, then these contradictions must be resolved by the management.

A meaningful operationalization of cultural change in the company can create a cascade of goals from the company's objectives to the executives to the employees. This cascade of goals is particularly helpful if it is decided on and tracked jointly with all stakeholders (see Fig. 3.14).

The ultimate goal of a data-centric corporate culture describes a paradigm shift. Employees and managers of the company no longer ask themselves the question: "What can we achieve with the system/application? But "What can we achieve with the data?" And with this philosophy, data-centric corporate culture paves the way for successful implementation of Data Governance. Of course, in reality, the transformation of corporate culture takes place in parallel with the implementation of Data

Fig. 3.14 Target cascade © Lars Michael Bollweg 2022. All Rights Reserved

Governance. But if this change in the way data is handled is accompanied not only on a professional level, but also on a cultural level, the chances of success are many times higher.

References

DAMA International (2017) DAMA-DMBOK: data management body of knowledge, 2nd edn. Technics Publications, New Jersey

Gascoigne H (2019) The business transformation playbook: how to implement your organization's target operating model (TOM). Hoba Tech, London

Ladley J (2012) Data governance: how to design, deploy and sustain an effective data governance program. Academic Press, Cambridge

Maydanchik A (2012) Data quality assessment. Technics Publications, New Jersey

McGilvray D (2008) Executing data quality projects: ten steps to quality data and trusted information. Morgan Kaufmann, Burlington

Plotkin D (2013) Data stewardship: an actionable guide to effective data management and data governance. Morgan Kaufmann, Burlington

Schein E, Schein P (2018) Organisationskultur und Leadership. Vahlen Verlag, München

Seiner R (2014) Non-invasive data governance: the path of least resistance and greatest success. Technics Publications, New Jersey

Templar M (2017) Get governed: building world class data governance programs. Ivory Lady Publishing, Wexford

Part III

Implement

Development of a Responsive Operating Model

4

Abstract

It is of great importance for the success of Data Governance that Data Governance and its processes within the company organization are understood and lived by all those involved. To achieve this, the company and its employees must not only internalize the processes, but also understand how the value contributions of Data Governance are made. Both points need to be explained and require correspondingly clear structures and process models. The development of an operating model for Data Governance provides the appropriate basis for this. In this chapter, we discuss the necessary basics of an operating model and show the different starting points for companies with a line or matrix organization. We then develop exemplary process models for the introduction and regular operation of Data Governance, thus creating a direct practical reference that you can transfer directly to the application of Data Governance.

4.1 Fundamentals of the Operating Model

An operating model serves both to support implementation and to ensure standardized processes for regular operation (Morrison 2021). The operating model for Data Governance describes in concrete terms how Data Governance delivers the added value promised to the company and which processes are necessary to achieve this. However, the name "operating model" can be misleading. It suggests that there must be an all-encompassing and integrating model that describes the operation of a company or a corporate function. In reality, however, an operating model is more of a collection of different models, visualizations, explanations, and process models that are interlinked to describe the operation of a corporate function. In this context, one also speaks of the documents of an operating model (Gascoigne 2019).

COMPONENTS OF THE OPERATING MODEL OF DATA GOVERNANCE	
1	**PROCEDURE MODEL / PROCESS PLANNING INTRODUCTION** STANDARD ACTIVITIES & SERVICES FOR THE INTRODUCTION OF DATA GOVERNANCE
2	**PROCEDURE MODEL / PROCESS PLANNING REGULAR OPERATION** STANDARD ACTIVITIES & SERVICES OF THE REGULAR OPERATION OF DATA GOVERNANCE

Accompanying the introduction of Data Governance, it is advisable to determine which documents are needed as support and then to create precisely these operating model documents.

> **Principle 22:** The Data Governance operating model is both a detailed visual and a detailed process description of the procedures of the Data Governance enterprise functions.

Based on experience, two documents have proven helpful as the basis for an operating model when introducing Data Governance: (1) **process model for introduction** and (2) **process model for regular operation**.

Whether further documents are required in the company depends on the individual case. In addition, but as an option to the process models mentioned, a communication and coordination model can also be developed on the basis of these process models, for example, as a basis for stakeholder management within the company.

The two basic forms of the operating model (Introduction and Regular Operation) are built on the Organizational Model (Centralized or Federated) and the Scaling Model (Use Case to Scale or Responsive Organization). It is important to understand that the operating model and the organizational and scaling model are much more complementary than they are distinct. The selection of the organizational scaling model creates the guardrails and landmarks for the operating model. The design of the operating model itself ensures that Data Governance's own processes mesh like cogs in the execution of tasks. The goal is to use the operating model to create a uniform approach for the introduction, operation, and further development of Data Governance (see Fig. 4.1).

The operating model goes beyond Data Management practices and, above all, includes collaboration with the business units (integration of business units). It is therefore tasked with ensuring dovetailing with the existing organizational structure and process organization in the company. To this end, the design of the organizational and scaling model must be unified with the company's organizational model that already exists in reality. This means that after the ideas for functioning Data Governance have been dealt with in theory, the operating model must be used to bring the theory into line with the practice of the company's reality.

In order to bring theory and practice together, it is necessary to delve into the advantages and disadvantages of the most common organizational forms with reference to the implementation of Data Governance. As a rule, one of two basic organizational forms is found in modern companies. On the one hand, there are companies that have a pure line organization in terms of both structure and process organization. On the other hand, there are companies that have expanded the line organization to include a matrix organization. Of course, there are also exotic and further mixed forms. But for the sake of simplicity, the focus here is on the most important and most frequently found organizational forms. However, conclusions can also be drawn from these to all other types of organizations.

4.2 Line Organization

In the classic line or functional organization, departments are formed that are staffed by several employees who handle tasks that are similar or interrelated. This is also where the term "functional organization" comes from. In the line organization, departments are structured and grouped together on a function-oriented basis (e.g., production, R&D, sales, and finance) (Morrison 2021) (see Fig. 4.2).

In the line organization, each employee has exactly one manager from whom he or she receives instructions. It is not uncommon that below the department heads/ managers there are no individual clerks hung up, but teams of employees, which in

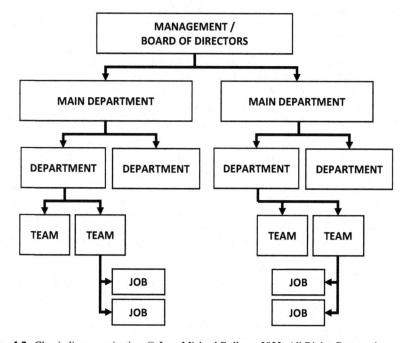

Fig. 4.2 Classic line organization © Lars Michael Bollweg 2022. All Rights Reserved

turn are coordinated and led by a team leader. This results in many hierarchical levels in the line organization, all with clear and well-defined areas of responsibility and competence, which are always managed and answered for by the next higher level. This hierarchical structure leads to the establishment of clear lines of service and decision-making within the company, which are followed by all employees in the organization. Although this makes it particularly easy for managers to control their teams and employees, the major disadvantage is that these long service and decision-making paths are associated with considerable delays and possible loss of information should interdepartmental coordination be necessary. A line organization makes cooperation between employees and departments more difficult and slows down developments because the ability to make decisions often depends solely on managers, who quickly form bottlenecks. As a result, the ability of employees to act is severely restricted by a lack of decision-making and directive authority, especially in dynamic projects. This can have a negative impact on cross-departmental digitalization projects in particular.

4.3   Matrix Organization

The structure of a matrix organization resembles a multi-line system. The matrix organization can also be understood as an extension of the line organization by a further dimension, which acts like a classic hierarchy with its management and directive competencies (Morrison 2021) (see Fig. 4.3).

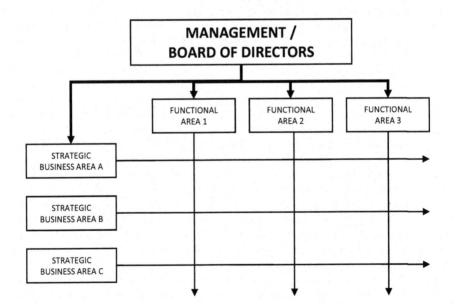

Fig. 4.3 Classic matrix organization © Lars Michael Bollweg 2022. All Rights Reserved

In the classic matrix organization, a distinction is made between two dimensions or areas: (1) **the functional areas,** such as production, purchasing, or sales; these are usually the departments of the line organization, and (2) **the product/process-related strategic business areas**; here one usually finds cross-departmental topics such as corporate processes, products, or projects that require a special form of attention from the company.

And exactly at the point where these two dimensions (functions and product/process-related strategic business units) intersect in the organization chart, there is either an employee or an entire team that takes on tasks both within the line and in the matrix. By organizing subject matter experts across departments (who, through the use of short communication channels and flat hierarchies within the company, can work efficiently with each other), the matrix achieves faster problem-solving. Furthermore, the End2End process view enabled by the matrix organization has a positive influence on the overarching process development (product quality, process quality, lead times, etc.), since all requirements for the process or product, including those beyond departmental boundaries, can be taken into account in the decisions and measures of the matrix organization. Furthermore, the relief of management through the delegation of management and decision-making competencies to the matrix is another positive side effect.

Of course, the matrix organization also brings disadvantages. In particular, the high communication effort and the crossover of competencies between the areas can lead to misunderstandings and problems in the process. In practice, this problem is often solved by assigning matrix and line responsibilities in one person. However, this problem can also be easily solved by means of a clear role design with clearly defined responsibilities and overarching coordination in the matrix.

4.4   Line or Matrix Organization

When implementing Data Governance, few data managers will be free to choose whether to implement in an existing line or matrix organization.

As a rule, one will have to accept this point as a given and come to terms with reality. However, if you are working in a company with a pure line organization, you at least have the chance to demonstrate the advantages of a matrix organization in the course of introducing Data Governance during the planning phase. However, the company must determine the right organizational form for itself and independently of Data Governance. Both organizational forms have a right to exist and can be right for different companies in different situations.

However, a company with a pure line organization has to pay the higher price from an organizational perspective when introducing Data Governance. Many activities that could actually be coordinated and harmonized across departments must ultimately be coordinated with each department individually. This creates a correspondingly greater need for coordination and, of course, greater personnel effort. However, since data and processes generally do not adhere to line organizations or departmental boundaries, the matrix organization is always preferable for setting up Data Governance. This is why we will continue to describe the introduction and development of the operating model using the example of a matrix organization. This form of organization is in any case predestined for the implementation of Data Governance, but it is expressly not a "must."

> **Principle 23:** Data Governance is most effectively implemented within a matrix organization. But classic line organizations also benefit from professional Data Management.

Data Governance can be implemented in any organizational form. And apart from the aspect of higher effort, which should not be underestimated, the procedure of Data Governance within a line organization is no different from the procedure of Data Governance within a matrix organization.

4.5   Procedure Model: Introduction of Data Governance

The establishment of Data Governance within a line organization is associated with greater organizational costs than a comparable establishment within a matrix organization. Nevertheless, the successful introduction of Data Governance is possible in both organizational forms. In neither organizational form is a so-called big bang, all changes at once, a sensible introduction procedure. It makes sense to start the introduction in small steps and to roll out Data Governance from the first successful implementations. So in the "Use Case to Scale" scaling model, implementation would classically start with a single use case, such as the implementation of the GDPR. And in the "Responsive Organization" scaling model, it would start with a single organizational building block, such as a process or a product.

Let's take a closer look at a concrete example of a "Responsive Organization." In the example, Data Governance is implemented within a matrix organization and along corporate processes. The introduction of Data Governance with this scaling model requires a two-stage process model.

The **first stage in the process model** describes the operationalization of the actual scaling model (see Fig. 4.4).

In the process model shown in Fig. 4.4, planning ("Design") is followed by four further phases in implementation. The implementation phase ("Implement") starts the development of the data organization with an implementation pilot, for example, a core process. If this pilot is successful, the data organization scales ("Scale") and develops the next "pilot" and then scales again until the entire company has been developed in this way.

It is important to emphasize, however, that the scaling model presented prescribes that Data Governance does not wait for the complete organizational setup, but takes up the activity of professional Data Management directly. Thus, whenever a pilot has been developed, according to the scaling model, this enterprise process can and

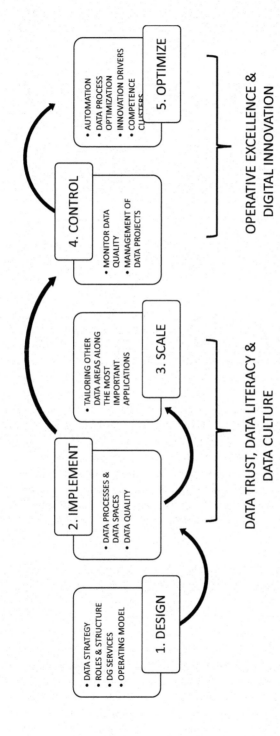

Fig. 4.4 Process model operationalization of the scaling model © Lars Michael Bollweg 2022. All Rights Reserved

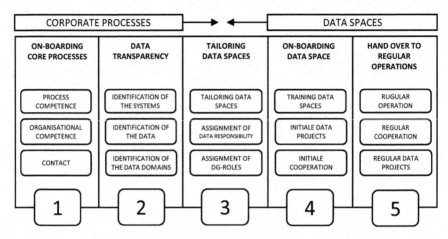

Fig. 4.5 5 Phase model introduction data governance © Lars Michael Bollweg 2022. All Rights Reserved

should already be controlled ("Control"), optimized ("Optimize"), and professionally managed by Data Governance. This accelerates the positive perception of the Data Governance program in the company and thus also the company's development in the context of the digital transformation.

The **second stage in the process model** describes the development of the individual pilots for the organizational structure. Here, too, a procedure in five phases is suitable for optimally designing the operational introduction (see Fig. 4.5).

The goal of the operational rollout and thus of the process model is to anchor the data space logic and the roles of Data Governance in the company and to hand them over to regular operations. This process is critical because it is decisive for the acceptance of the change within the company. In the end, people are affected by the introduction of Data Governance, and they must be informed as best as possible about the change and empowered to deal with it. This is true for every change process and therefore also for the introduction of Data Governance. The following phases take this challenge into account and address it consciously.

1. On-Boarding

In the first phase of the operational rollout in a pilot, the aim is to develop three milestones: (1) process competence, (2) organizational competence, and (3) contacts and network.

Process competence: At the very beginning, it is important to ensure that the Data Management staff responsible for introducing Data Governance and the other roles within Data Governance can be perceived as competent contacts in the organization of corporate processes. To achieve this, it is important to invest in the know-how of the respective employees about the corporate process. Data Governance employees must know and understand the individual activities and work steps of the enterprise process from the very beginning. When developing process expertise, it makes direct sense to also focus on pain points and process challenges as well as upcoming new developments. This phase of familiarization also allows data experts to directly identify the issues that the business units are currently working on. In this way, the Data Governance roles can get involved in the process work right from the start with precisely tailored development and optimization proposals.

Organizational competency: After the Data Governance team has gained an understanding of the process, it is important to also gain a clear understanding of the organization of the enterprise process. In detail, this involves questions such as: What are the standard deadlines? How are decisions made in the process team? And, of course, always: What problems are there in the organization right now and what pain points are particularly pressing for the organization? This information is important in order to be alerted particularly early on to any communication or coordination problems that could be critical to the implementation success of Data Governance.

Contact persons and network: The final milestone in on-boarding is the establishment of a functioning network of competent contact persons around the corporate process. In many companies, the contact between the process organization (often process management) and Data Management serves as a starting point. In addition, regular participation in regular meetings of the process organization acts as a driver for the network. On the one hand, this point is important in order to make the transition to the regular process as smooth as possible, but it is also direct groundwork for filling the Data Governance roles. As a rule, data-related topics are already being dealt with in detail by colleagues within the processes. These colleagues must be identified and documented in Data Governance, e.g., as subject matter experts.

On-boarding Data Governance into enterprise process structures may well take 14 days, as it is important to understand the core process in depth and to be able to track the process activities that process staff perform operationally.

2. Data Transparency

For Data Management, it is crucial in this second implementation phase to analyze the previously learned core process in more detail at the IT and data and data domain level. To this end, three milestones are developed in this phase: (1) identification of the systems, (2) identification of the data, and (3) identification of the data domains.

Identification of the systems: The basis for professional Data Management is the identification of the IT systems involved. This task sounds trivial, but it is a real challenge, especially when including so-called shadow IT (IT systems that are used in the business departments without the knowledge of the IT department). This task must be completed comprehensively because the systems and databases used within the process define the boundaries for the data to be considered. Thus, the systems create the initial boundary for the data domains. In order to comprehensively identify the IT systems, the contacts identified in the first phase are of great importance. Of course, it makes sense to document all identified systems.

Identification of the data: The identification of the systems is followed by the first examination of the data of the process. In accordance with the CRUD logic presented, it is examined which data within the systems is created, used, maintained,

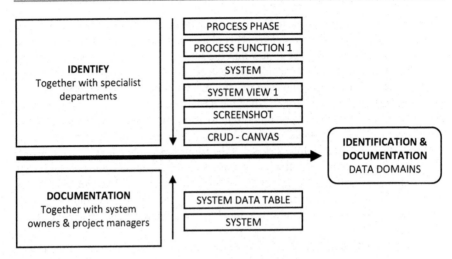

Fig. 4.6 Identification of data domains © Lars Michael Bollweg 2022. All Rights Reserved

and deleted by employees of the process. The data that is created by the process is of particular importance because, in terms of Data Governance, the enterprise process has data responsibility for this data, even toward other users of the data from other processes. In addition, any data that is used by the process but not created by the process itself is also of great importance because the process is the requester of the data here and must communicate with the creator about its own requirements for the data. Following this step, it is also useful to document the knowledge gained or data determined for the respective IT system (see Fig. 4.6).

Identification of data domains: Finally, the documented data must be classified and grouped into a data domain. This means that similar data is grouped into clusters. This simplification or reduction in complexity allows the data domain to communicate on a management level about its own data and thereby manage the data of the data domain more efficiently and effectively. Examples of useful data domains include "order data" or "documentation data"; these collective terms then group together all the data relating to an order that has been created or to the creation of documentation.

3. Trim Data Spaces

The third phase builds on the first two phases. In this phase, the actual course is set for the data organization. Together with the process organization, the identified contact persons and the documentation of IT systems and data domains that has been created, the data spaces are tailored and filled with the Data Governance roles. Again, three milestones are developed for this: (1) tailoring the data spaces, (2) assigning data responsibility, and (3) assigning the Data Governance roles.

Trimming the data spaces: Using the information about the data obtained in the previous phase of data transparency, the data range(s) are trimmed. It is recommended to keep the number of data spaces as small as possible. The

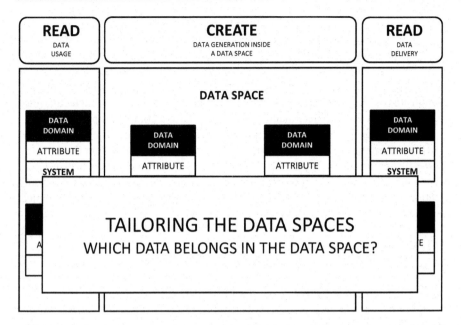

Fig. 4.7 Trimming data spaces © Lars Michael Bollweg 2022. All Rights Reserved

boundaries of the data spaces define the systems; the contents of the data spaces define the CRUD logic. To simplify the management of the data spaces and stakeholder communication, the contents of the data spaces should be clustered into data domains (see Fig. 4.7).

Assignment of data responsibility: The role of the person responsible for the data is usually set directly from the hierarchy of the organization due to the creator principle. That is, it makes sense for an executive from top management to be data responsible, i.e., the data owner. The data owner role is a strategic role and is represented operationally by the data steward. Alternative models for distributing data responsibility, so-called political models, are usually not effective because they are often not comprehensible to the organization. In some companies, data responsibility is also assigned to operational employees. However, these employees are not able to make strategic decisions on how to deal with data and therefore often do no more than perform pure "maintenance tasks." At the strategic level, these companies usually remain unable to act or are at least limited in their capabilities.

Assignment of Data Governance roles: Assigning Data Governance roles is one of the biggest challenges in establishing Data Governance. While some roles are easy to fill, e.g., like the data owner or the subject matter and technical data experts, because they are only brought in strategically or in an advisory capacity, other roles are more difficult to fill because the organization must provide the resources for these roles, which usually requires a not inconsiderable amount of convincing in any organization.

In any case, one of the more difficult roles to fill is the data steward, as this employee must take on the most new tasks and the skill profile is demanding.

The other roles, such as the data project manager and IT administrator, are usually filled before Data Governance is implemented.

Of course, in processes with multiple systems, there can easily be multiple IT administrators (one for each system) or multiple subject matter and factual data experts (one for each subject matter topic/multiple for a complex topic).

The following phases (4) and (5) are of particular importance. They represent the transition from the organizational setup to the regular operation of Data Governance. These phases are described briefly below. However, in order to do justice to the importance of regular operation in particular, it is necessary to go into greater detail. Section 4.6 is therefore devoted to these two phases again in detail. And the complete fourth part of this book takes another look at regular operation with all its facets.

4. Train Data Spaces

Once the data space has been tailored and staffed with Data Governance roles, it is important that the newly created data organization is not left to its own devices. Employees must be informed about the tasks that will be assigned to them. They must be trained and empowered in the topics in which they are not trained. To accomplish this, three milestones are developed in this phase: (1) training of data spaces, (2) initial data projects, and (3) initial coordination with other data spaces.

Training of data spaces: The training of the data spaces primarily consists of enabling the employees who assume Data Governance roles to be able to execute them professionally. For this purpose, both the Data Governance processes and the Data Management practices should be part of the training.

Initial data projects: Since training can only ever be a basis for experience in real projects, it makes sense to have the initial data projects within the data spaces accompanied very intensively by the Data Governance office, thus helping the roles within the accompaniment to shape the transfer from theory to practice. It often also makes sense to closely accompany the initial identification of data projects to ensure that the topic potentials are correctly identified. This phase is not a foregone conclusion. It needs intensive attention for a longer period of time, and it is important that there is a regular exchange between those responsible in order to keep up to date on the status of the work and satisfaction with implementation.

Initial coordination with other data spaces: The final step that should be accompanied within the implementation phase of the data spaces is the exchange between the data spaces. Data spaces are always in a relationship when they mutually exchange data with each other or further develop common processes or systems. When exchanging data, exactly one data space is always "data responsible" (the data space that generates the data), and one or more data spaces are "data requesters," i.e., a data space that uses the data generated in another data space. Both sides have "responsibilities" within this relationship. The data space that generates the data is responsible for creating the data in a way that is appropriate for its use throughout the data lifecycle, including the use of the data by subsequent data spaces. The data requesting data spaces are responsible for documenting their data requirements and communicating them to the generating data space. This interplay in the exchange of data spaces means a deep cultural change for many companies and requires close initial support in any case.

5. Regular Operation of the Data Spaces
In the last phase, the data space has reached a level of maturity where the Data Governance office no longer needs to be actively and operationally involved in the management of the data. The Data Governance office can focus more on its strategic and enabling role from this stage. The data space has reached this level of maturity when it has established the following Data Governance foundations: (1) regular operation data space, (2) regular reconciliation, and (3) regular data projects.

Regular operation of the data space: This point is usually reached after about 4 months of setting up the data organization and is decided together with the Data Governance roles that have been filled.

Regular reconciliations: The data space recognizes that the maturity level for regular operation has been reached when it is anchored within the process organization and the exchange with the adjacent data spaces has been internalized.

Regular data projects: The operational value-added strategy recommends permanent processing of data projects. These data projects fuel regular operations and, by their very nature (projects create challenges—challenges overcome create experience), create leaps in development in terms of the maturity of a data space.

> **Principle 24:** Implement Data Governance in five stages: (1) on-boarding, (2) establishing data transparency, (3) tailoring data spaces and staff roles, (4) empowering data spaces, and (5) initiating regular operation.

The implementation of a data space in the company thus ends when the data space has taken up a steady work rhythm for the implementation of data projects. Parallel to this maturity level, a change to the process model of regular operation takes place.

4.6   Procedure Model: Preparation for Regular Operation of Data Governance

Transitioning to and maintaining the regular operation of Data Governance is a similarly complex and challenging activity as implementing Data Governance.

Regular operation begins after a data space has been tailored, the data domains (roughly) defined, and data responsibility assigned. In addition, regular data projects are already identified and implemented at this point. Ideally, the data space is also already controlled via a project or process organization within the matrix organization or via a specialist department within the line organization of a company. This means that the data space is already anchored in the matrix or line and the specialist department integration has been successfully completed within the implementation phase.

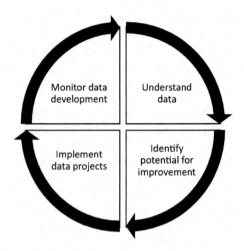

The transition to regular operation is a significant turning point in the implementation of Data Governance. At this point, the organizational setup ends and the actual data work begins, i.e., the value creation of the data within the organization.

Unfortunately, like all implementation steps in building Data Governance, this one is not a no-brainer. The employees who are to fill the roles of Data Governance and the employees who support the roles are usually inexperienced in the practices of Data Management and still need to be empowered to perform the tasks at hand (see also Sects. 2.6 Structures of Data Governance, 3.3 Developing Data Management Capabilities, 4.5 Procedure model: Introduction of Data Governance, and 4.6 Procedure model: Preparation for regular operation of a Data Governance).

The tasks that Data Governance roles must perform as a standard activity to manage data spaces are diverse, and the thematic focus for performing these tasks varies from company to company. However, they generally fall into one of the following four categories: (1) understand data, (2) identify pain points and areas for improvement, (3) implement data projects, and (4) monitor data development (see Fig. 4.8).

These categories reflect the regular operation of Data Governance and, with it, the tasks that are assigned to Data Governance roles and for which employees must be prepared. In the following, the four categories will be examined in greater depth using exemplary tasks in order to gain a better understanding of each individual category and the underlying operational work within Data Governance.

Understand Data

The following tasks fall into the category "**Understanding data**" as examples:

Cataloging data: The first step of data cataloging deals with the actual collection of the relevant data for a data space. That is, with answering the question, what data are we responsible for? What data do we use? And in which databases is this data located?

Data cataloging is one of the most fundamental activities for Data Management of data spaces. Without knowledge of the data to be managed and monitored by a data space, professional Data Management is not possible. The introduction of an enterprise-wide data catalog, usually accessible as a web app, can be a useful addition for this task. A data catalog has the advantage that the knowledge acquired in the data space can be made accessible to the entire company via the data catalog. In many companies, however, cataloging is still done in Excel spreadsheets. This is not really recommended, but as a low-budget variant it is still better than not having any information at all about the data to be managed.

Once it has been determined which data is managed in a data space, the second step is to expand this data with data definitions. This means that the purely quantitative information (What data is available? Number, location) is supplemented by initial qualitative information (What does the data mean?). For the definition of data, a structured approach is a good choice. A comprehensive template for a structured data definition can be found in the appendix.

Document data lineage: In addition to the pure information about what data is available, the data flow is the most important information that is necessary for the professional management of data. The data flow, i.e., the trace of the data within the system landscapes, is also called data lineage. The documentation of this data lineage shows at which location (e.g., in which database of which system) a data was generated and via which interfaces it is passed on in the system landscape of a company. The documentation of a data lineage can be thought of as a map of a subway network in a large city. The direction of flow of the individual data is shown in lines between the individual stops (systems). This allows one to trace the spread of a piece of information and also to assess its influence on downstream systems. So one can decide for oneself where to start in the data flow and begin with the optimization. Of course, the starting point of a data lifecycle, i.e., the generation, is always recommended for the beginning of an optimization. But when a data lifecycle really begins is not always as clear as one would like to wish and imagine in theory. To get clarity on such questions, a documented data lineage is invaluable.

Classify data: The classification of data is, on the one hand, in the greatest interest of a company and, on the other hand, an activity that the legislator has ordered the company to do, so it is something that must be done.

The interest of companies in classifying data is easy to explain: a company wants to know what data is important. What data has a critical impact on how the business can be run? And what data would incur significant costs to recover if it were lost or unintentionally altered?

On the other hand, the legislator requires companies, among other things, to provide special protection for personal data and to delete it after the end of the purpose limitation and the retention periods. Classification is necessary for both.

In purely practical terms, this means that the company data is tagged as part of a data classification process (e.g., "Critical data," "Personal data"), i.e., the data is assigned to a specific class or group. A data catalog also lends itself to supporting and documenting this activity.

REVENUE-RELATED VALUATIONS INCOME APPROACH	COST-RELATED VALUATIONS COST APPROACH	IMPACT-RELATED VALUATIONS MARKET APPROACH
• Contribution or lost contribution to company profit	• Costs data generation/ data maintenance • Costs of data recovery • Damage assessment in case of incorrect/ missing data	• Influence on the strategic development of the company • Willingness to pay for license costs in case of missing data

Fig. 4.9 Data evaluation approaches © Lars Michael Bollweg 2022. All Rights Reserved

Valuing data: Data valuation is one of the basic approaches to data classification. Three approaches are usually used for data valuation: (1) revenue-based approaches, (2) cost-based approaches, and (3) impact-based approaches (see Fig. 4.9).

Revenue-based approaches deal with the contribution or forgone contribution that data makes to a company's bottom line. This type of data assessment is thus directly oriented to revenue or sales.

The cost-based approaches value data in terms of the costs incurred to create, modify, or delete that data. Often, these approaches also include the cost of recovering lost data or damage estimates for the costs that may be incurred if data is lost or compromised.

The impact-related approaches to data evaluation deal with the strategic importance of data, for example, for future fields such as artificial intelligence. Another variant, however, also deals, for example, with how great a company's willingness to pay would be if certain data were not available and had to be purchased by license.

All these assessments are followed by evaluations, which can then again be the basis for data classification.

Identify Pain Points and Potentials
The following tasks fall into the category "**Identify pain points and potentials**" as examples:

Document data requirements: A classic activity for identifying pain points and potentials is the structured discussion of existing requirements for data in the company. By discussing what data should actually do and what it is capable of doing in reality, it is very easy to identify existing pain points. Accordingly, the professionalization of data requirements documentation holds very great potential for the further development of a company. Possible formats for gathering data requirements include 1:1 expert interviews, workshops, and surveys. In terms of methodology, process-oriented system models are suitable for requirements gathering and processing.

Consider future developments: The sole consideration of existing data requirements only puts a company in the position of optimizing the ACTUAL. But real further developments within processes and IT systems often require a complete change of the ACTUAL states (disruption). However, disruptive business potentials cannot be derived from the existing requirements for the ACTUAL states, but require a broader view beyond the end of one's nose. For example, there is no point in continuing to optimize internal combustion engines if their approval is restricted by the legislature and customer demand in the future will only be for electric motors.

Therefore, the question "What data will we need in 3 to 5 years?" is part of the standard repertoire of data project managers and data space officers.

The question about future developments in the medium term can usually be answered very well today, since the developments that will be ready for the market in 3 to 5 years are already being discussed in the trade press and piloted in the industry. The future is therefore a subject area for which one should already prepare today.

The identification of pain points and potentials is also discussed in more detail in Sect. 6.3, Data-driven value stream optimization.

Implement Data Projects
The following tasks fall into the category **"Implement data projects"** as examples:

Optimize data generation: A classic optimization of data quality is the optimization of the generation of data. This usually means optimizing the data input. There are a variety of simple to complex solutions for optimizing data generation. A standard procedure, for example, is the replacement or exchange of free text fields by drop-down or other predefined selection fields within user dialogs in the frontend. In addition, input validations are often used to standardize certain inputs, such as address data, or to ensure their completeness.

Optimize data maintenance: Optimizing data maintenance is a similar approach. Here, it is a matter of ensuring that the employees who are entrusted with changing or maintaining existing data (e.g., supplementing, correcting) are also supported in this activity by the system, if necessary through (partial) automation. The further development of user dialogs and the use of validations are also usually the means of choice for optimizing data maintenance.

Optimize data usage: There are always two options for optimizing data usage. Either you adapt the data to the requirements of the users (certainly the most common and best case) or you adapt the use of the data to the state of the data.

Fulfilling the first case is the primary goal of professional Data Management. Data quality must fit the requirements. But sometimes it is not possible to change existing data.

The second case therefore always occurs when data cannot be adapted to user requirements, or only at great expense/effort.

In this fortunately rare case, the task of educating and training data users falls to the data organization. This possibility, though unpopular with most data professionals, should always be explored as an option by Data Management, as changing data usage can also enable the achievement of business goals. And as has been pointed out several times at the beginning of this book, the real purpose of Data Governance and professional management of data is to achieve business goals.

Optimize data architecture: In addition to how data is generated, there is always the question of what data should be generated or captured. And every extension of data generation and data capture leads to an adaptation of the data architectures. In other words, the extension or reduction of data structures (tables, documents, etc.) forces the data architecture to change. These changes to data architectures are standard Data Management activities and reflect the responsiveness and maturity of a data organization. If, for example, the extension of a data object "Addresses" by a new column, e.g., "Floor," is only feasible at great expense to the company, then this indicates a low level of maturity and low responsiveness of the data organization. At the same time, this indicates a potential for further development and improvement for the data organization and the entire company.

Monitor Data Development

The category **"Monitor data development" includes** exemplary tasks from the area of data quality management:

Monitoring data quality: Data quality monitoring is the supreme discipline in the regular operation of Data Governance. It takes the management of data from a reactive state to a proactive one. This means that as soon as a company begins to actively monitor its data, it is in a position to optimize this data proactively, i.e., before data problems occur (see Fig. 4.10).

CATALOG DATA	DOCUMENT DATA LINEAGE	MONITOR DATA QUALITY
IMPROVE DATA QUALITY	COMMUNICATE DATA QUALITY	CLASSIFY & EVALUATE DATA
OPTIMIZE DATA GENERATION	OPTIMIZE DATA MAINTENANCE	OPTIMIZE DATA USE
OPTIMIZE DATA ARCHITECTURE	DOCUMENT DATA REQUIREMENTS	TAKE FUTURE DEVELOPMENTS INTO ACCOUNT

Fig. 4.11 Tasks in the regular operation of Data Governance © Lars Michael Bollweg 2022. All Rights Reserved

Dashboards can be used to visualize data monitoring, which can also be made available to management and thus also used as a communication medium for the development status of Data Governance.

The "data monitoring" phase is followed by the "data understanding" phase. Monitored data must be classified again and optimized according to new identified data requirements. The eternal cycle begins and the continuous improvement process is established.

Principle 25: The regular operation of Data Governance is a cycle of (1) understanding data, (2) identifying pain points and areas for improvement, (3) implementing data projects, and (4) monitoring data development.

Overview of exemplary tasks for the regular operation of Data Governance (see Fig. 4.11):

The regular operation of Data Governance is therefore visibly accompanied by a large number of tasks that cannot be handled by a company without additional effort. This poses a challenge for many companies, as they tend to let Data Management fall by the wayside as a secondary activity in their resource planning. However, investing in Data Management is an investment in the future viability of the company – and therefore a necessary one.

The employees who fill the roles of Data Governance are automatically integrated into a continuous improvement process through the tasks in the regular operation of a Data Governance and, in parallel, positively influence the corporate culture in dealing with data as a whole as multipliers. But of course, the management of such a change process is always accompanied by a variety of challenges. Among the biggest of these are the structured identification and prioritization of data projects to ensure that Data Governance is also working on the right things. How to methodically and practically address these and other challenges of the regular operation of a Data Governance is explained in the following fourth part.

References

Gascoigne H (2019) The business transformation playbook: how to implement your organization's target operating model (TOM). Hoba Tech, London

Morrison R (2021) Data-driven organization design: delivering perpetual performance gains through the organizational system. Kogan Page, London

Part IV

Run

Fundamentals of the Digital Transformation

5

Abstract

The previous chapters of this book have focused on the organizational structure of Data Governance and the professionalization of Data Management. It has already been shown many times that modern Data Governance can be much more powerful than just professionally managing the creation, use, maintenance, and deletion of data. In this fourth part and the following chapters, after a theoretical foundation, it will be shown in very practical terms how the services of Data Governance anchored in the company's business architecture can be used, e.g., with the help of data-driven value stream optimization as a driver for the digital transformation of a company.

The term "digital transformation" as used in this book describes the continuous optimization and further development of the digital tools that the company uses to achieve its goals.

> **Principle 26:** Digital transformation is the continuous optimization and further development of digital tools in the company.

Continuous optimization and the ongoing identification of potential requirements for digital tools is the real challenge for companies. But it is a challenge that can be operationalized with the help of structured methods. Companies must enable their organization to transform digital transformation from an abstract fashionable concept into a plannable, structured, and calculable corporate function. The following chapters lay the foundation for this and also delve into how well-planned Data Governance can support the company in solving this challenge.

© Springer-Verlag GmbH Germany, part of Springer Nature 2022
L. M. Bollweg, *Data Governance for Managers*, Management for Professionals,
https://doi.org/10.1007/978-3-662-65171-1_5

5.1   Stages of Digital Value Creation

The terms "Data Governance" and "digital transformation" are not only thematically related, but also have in common that many people do not have a clear idea of what they really mean and how they can make them practically useful for themselves and their companies.

At this point in the book, however, at least all readers who have made it this far should have gained a clear idea of what Data Governance is and what Data Governance can do for a company. In this and the following chapters, the knowledge gained so far will be supplemented, and based on the challenges of digital transformation, it will be shown how Data Governance can deliver further cross-data added value for companies in the context of data-driven developments.

By the end of this chapter, the term "digital transformation" should also have lost its vagueness and the tasks facing companies in the context of digital transformation should be tangible.

One of the most important strategies in dealing with data and digital developments as a whole is complexity reduction: in other words, the simplification of complicated reality. And even when thinking about the value creation potential of digital transformation, it makes sense to start with simplification first. That is why the following section first describes the meta-level of the individual value creation stages of digitalization before we delve further into the complex depths of digital reality.

A digital value stage in the context of digital transformation is very similar to an operational value stage in manufacturing companies, i.e., in the sense of a finishing stage. A valuable product is produced along each digital value creation stage. The more stages a digital product has passed through or skipped, the more refinements have been carried out and the higher its subsequent value.

In theory, five digital or data-driven stages of value creation can be distinguished: (1) data collection and preparation, (2) dashboards and statistics, (3) pattern recognition and early warning systems, (4) process development and flow improvements, and (5) automation (Hadaya and Gagnon 2017) (see Fig. 5.1).

It is worth delving deeper here because thinking in terms of digital value creation stages is unfamiliar to many companies. As already mentioned, each of these five digital value creation stages in itself already forms the framework for a digital product. The more digital value creation stages the digital product has passed through or skipped, the more valuable it is. So while a digital product at the lowest value creation stage may still consist of a single Excel file, a digital product at the highest value creation stage is usually part of a complex software development. However, the world of digital developments is not black and white. There are plenty of shades of gray and transitions. That is why it is valuable to delve into the broad framework of digital value creation along the stages presented, but not as a final categorization, but rather as a guardrail for classifying the multilayered reality on the highway of possibilities.

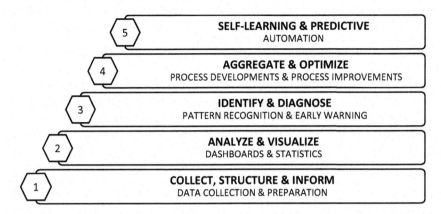

Fig. 5.1 The five stages of data value creation © Lars Michael Bollweg 2022. All Rights Reserved

(1) Data Collection and Preparation

At the lowest level of the five digital value creation stages is **"data collection and preparation."** At this level, digitalization or data value creation does no more than simply capture and store data and then present the information contained therein, often descriptively. This is usually done within the widely established simple office (e.g., Word, Excel) and database systems (Access, MySQL, etc.). This most rudimentary process of data processing is the basis for all subsequent digital value creation stages and naturally generates added value in itself. Companies have been using this lowest level of value creation for communication and decision support for many decades—and across almost all sectors and industries. True to the motto: Only those who collect data can also utilize it.

(2) Dashboards and Statistics

The second stage, **"dashboards and statistics,"** already prepares for a first deeper exploitation of the information via the statistical evaluation and the subsequent visualization and presentation of the information on dashboards, e.g., within a BI tool or a web app. The statistical evaluations supplement the previously collected data with additional, often visually accessible information that was invisible before further evaluation. This process is also described as the first "enrichment of the data" or "refinement" because the added value of the data after the analysis and evaluation performed is higher than in the previous raw state. Second-stage data enrichment often occurs simply by transforming the raw data into visualizations such as maps, graphs, charts, and the like. The deeper use of algorithms is possible at this stage, but not yet the norm. A greater impact on the new value gained for the company at this stage of the value chain is the dissemination of the processed information via dashboards. The expansion of the data user group via the easy accessibility of the information, e.g., via the company intranet, leads to positive dispersion effects within the organization. True to the motto: knowledge is power and power enables change.

(3) Pattern Recognition and Early Warning Systems
The lowest two levels of digital value creation are the most common types of data value creation in traditional companies. They are still very much characterized by manual interventions, and their influence on the physical process chains, i.e., the direct value creation in the company, is low. The situation is already different at the third value creation stage **"pattern recognition and early warnings."** At this stage, the first partial automation occurs within simple IT systems. With the help of these simple systems, processed data is examined and early warnings, so-called alerts, are generated based on defined threshold values or by means of pattern recognition through algorithms. These early warnings or alerts enable the systems to call their users to physical action: in other words, call the user to actively intervene in the processes of the physical or technical process chains. An action triggered in this way can just as easily be the removal of a defective product on the production line as the correction of an incorrect key figure on the annual report. The third value creation stage is therefore characterized by a system triggering the actions of a human user in the sense of a digital assistant. However, the triggered action itself has not changed particularly much as a result of digitalization. It is generally still the same action that would have been performed if it had been triggered by a human. In the case of stage three value creation, humans often still serve as a corrective to the digital impetus for action. Further examples of value creation at this level are the system-based warning of a suspicious transaction or the warning of a production line overheating. After both "early warnings," a human being will evaluate these system-generated indications once again and only then draw consequences, e.g., block the transaction or shut down the production line. True to the motto: What you do not check yourself has not happened.

(4) Process Development and Process Improvements
The fourth stage of digital value creation, **"process development and process improvements,"** builds on the previous stages. Physical actions are also triggered by digital impulses at the fourth stage. The only difference is that the actions triggered at this stage of the value chain have already been profoundly changed by the digital data streams. In concrete terms, this means that the use of digital systems and digital products at this stage of the value chain has already changed the physical processes, i.e., the type and sequence of physical actions in a process chain. Examples of this are smart contracts (digital contracts), which make the physical sending of documents superfluous, or RFID chips, which can replace the performance of a manual annual inventory with an automated, scanner-supported inventory in real time.

As a rule, partial automation is achieved at the fourth stage of the value chain, reducing and aggregating the number of physical actions, i.e., increasing productivity and thus improving the process. In some cases, the nature of the physical actions is already completely changed. Thus, completely different actions and activities become necessary for process fulfillment. Imagine the work in a wage tax assistance association. Twenty years ago, this was completely paper based; today, software solutions assist in filling out and sending income tax forms. In fact, the software today is so good that the need for income tax assistance associations as a whole can at least be questioned. So in some cases, the changes at the fourth stage are so extensive that it is at this stage of the value chain that we first encounter the term "disruption"—the complete redesign of a process. True to the motto: breaking new ground.

(5) Automation
The final stage of digital value creation, **"automation,"** is the actual goal of digitalization: the complete mapping of a process via a digital information flow—without any manual intervention.

Process automation is often only made possible by robotics, sensor technology, or other digitally controlled machine support. In classic companies, automation was primarily aimed at eliminating labor costs, i.e., replacing manual work with machine work. In the context of digital transformation, this view has evolved. The automation generated by digitalization naturally also aims to replace physical processes with digital processes. But in addition, digital processes and products have a decisive advantage over machine-automated physical processes. With closed "digital" information chains, you benefit from their scalability at virtually the same cost (zero copy cost). This means that digital processes and products only generate costs or expenses "once" during creation; for each additional copy, for each additional run, only minimal operating expenses are then generated. The contribution margin is almost 100%.

At this top level of digital value creation, algorithms from the spectrum of artificial intelligence, in particular from the field of machine learning, are frequently used to solve complex decision-making processes along demanding workflows. These "self-learning" algorithms enable companies to digitize and thus automate even very challenging processes that are heavily dependent on expert knowledge. Examples include a large number of processes that are already anchored in everyday life, such as ordering via online stores, listening to digital music, the paperless office, and many more. True to the motto: What I don't have to do myself, I'm happy to do.

The fundamental knowledge of these value creation stages is of great importance for every role within Data Governance because it is the basis for recognizing and evaluating potential data projects. This means that the digital value creation stages can be viewed as a planning and decision-making aid. They support every employee in assessing whether certain measures that a company is planning with regard to digital transformation will also generate the greatest possible effect, the greatest possible added value, and move the company forward or merely maintain the status quo.

In practical terms, the value creation levels can be used as a target corridor for project planning and the identification of IT development potential. It is possible to make a concrete assessment of whether data projects are at the lowest levels of the value chain (1–2) and thus bring little change (little digital development), or whether they enable partial or full automation (3–5) and thus fundamentally change work and action in the company (digital transformation).

> **Principle 27:** The five digital value creation stages serve as a compass and support for the target planning of data-driven development projects.

With knowledge of the digital value creation stages, the view of digital transformation should have changed from an abstract description to a concrete consideration of measures along precisely these presented value creation stages. However, knowledge of the digital value creation stages is only one part of adding value to the digital transformation in the company with the help of Data Governance. The other, often even more decisive part, is the ability to identify digital business needs: in other words, the ability to concretely identify IT requirements to support the workflows and processes in the company and thus also the ability to identify the digital development potential as part of data-driven process optimization.

As with all challenges of professional Data Management, the key to data-driven process optimization lies in close cooperation between the units along the dimensions of "processes, data, and IT systems."

In other words, for Data Governance to be an effective driver of digitalization in a company, it must work closely with the units that plan and design the processes and IT systems.

In the next chapter, we will take a closer look at these three areas again before turning to the concrete methods and approach for data-driven process development.

5.2   Fundamentals of Business Architecture

The power of Data Governance to drive digital transformation is a particularly exciting aspect of professional Data Management. Unfortunately, the phrase "Data Governance as a driver of digital transformation" is often misinterpreted in this context. By "Data Governance as a driver..." is meant neither "Data Governance alone," "Data Governance as the sole implementer," nor "Data Governance as the only necessary unit for corporate happiness." Data Governance is always only a small part of the overall activities of all corporate units and works best as a "proactive service provider" with all other units and areas in the company.

But let's start from the beginning again: If a company has accepted digital transformation as a challenge, then the question arises as to how this task is operationalized and anchored in the company. Often, digitalization officers are appointed or entire departments are created with the task of "digitalization." These roles and units work with the departments to find potential digitalization projects and develop them within pilots and roadmaps all the way to implementation. Some of these projects fail, while others are successful. This is normal and an expression of an ongoing development—the digital transformation.

The problem, however, is that the digitalization task and the responsibility for digitalization are outsourced from the specialist departments to these roles and departments. This means that in this constellation, the departments are "digitized"

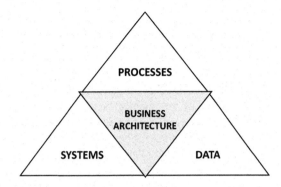

from the outside, as it were. This "external" solution to the digitalization task is also reflected in the adaptation of the digital tools by the employees and thus also in the corporate culture that is lived out: "Digitalization is a task for others. I myself, as an employee, cannot make a contribution. What I need in terms of digital tools is provided for me."

This "passive" attitude to digitalization often arises among employees when departments and specialist areas are supposed to change, but do not help develop and commission the changes themselves. The employees in these "externally" digitized units are then always subject in one way or another to "outside forces" with which they must come to terms. The feeling of being externally determined almost inevitably leads to resistance among employees. Barriers to development arise. Often rightly so, because without the involvement of the employees, the best solution for an existing problem or task can rarely be found.

The most successful way to implement change in companies and organizations is always to involve those affected in the change process. This still does not ensure that the best digital solutions have been identified. We'll get to how to identify them in the next chapter. But you make sure that you have all your employees on board and that you have their support. And that is sometimes even more important than having the very best solution in place.

The operationalization of digital transformation therefore has a large change management component simply because of the high speed of change, and the success of digital development depends in no small measure on the corporate culture developed over the years and decades.

This is where the circle closes; Data Governance implemented in the corporate organization has the best prerequisites for driving change processes from "within" and anchoring the constant change in dealing with digital tools deeply in the corporate culture.

However, Data Governance is only one voice color in the triad of processes, data, and systems—i.e., only one voice color in the so-called business architecture (Kotusev 2018; Bente 2012) (see Fig. 5.2).

Without collaboration along the business architecture, processes, and IT systems, even the value proposition of Data Governance would not be sufficient to drive digital transformation in the enterprise. It is this co-dependency between data, processes, and systems that makes digital transformation so challenging for companies (Yildiz 2019). But it is also the view of this co-dependency that enables companies to identify digital value creation potential, such as for automation.

> **Principle 28:** Data Governance as a Data Management tool is a fundamental component of the business architecture. But Data Governance is only one important component of three. Data Governance complements process and IT system management in the business architecture to provide a unified view of data, processes, and IT systems.

In the following, we will once again go into detail about the collaboration potential of Data Governance with the units around processes (e.g., process management, process optimization, process development) and IT (IT management, IT architecture, IT development). And it will become comprehensible what is really meant by the saying "Data Governance as a driver of digital transformation," namely, "Data Governance as a driver of interface development between processes and IT."

Of course, Data Management and thus Data Governance work successfully with all units within the company. But especially in view of the challenges of digital transformation, out of the multitude of departments and areas within companies, cooperation with processes and IT has proven to be particularly valuable for the success of Data Governance and thus also for its role as a driver of digital transformation. Close collaboration between processes, data, and IT systems is therefore particularly valuable, as all three have a supporting mission for the target fulfillment of the company's core processes and are dependent on each other for service delivery. Data lives in IT systems, IT systems, and data serve the process, and the process uses data and IT systems to fulfill the company goals.

It is the special role that data plays in the web of relationships and at the interfaces between processes and IT that makes the leverage of Data Governance visible: To understand data, you have to understand the process, and to develop data, you have to understand the systems. When the perspectives of processes and IT systems are united with the data perspective of Data Governance, they result in the complete blueprint of the company and thus an unobstructed view of the digital development potential.

EXCURSUS: The discipline of business architecture is in a relationship with its sister or twin discipline "enterprise architecture" that has not been clarified by science and practice. We will not be able to resolve this monster of vagueness in terms of overlapping and then delimiting concepts, objectives, tools, and methods in this book either (see Fig. 5.3).

Therefore, for common understanding in this book, we delineate this term "business architecture" as follows:

Business architecture, and thus business architecture management, pursues the goal of data, process, and system harmonization. To this end, the corporate goals formulated by the company's management are translated by business architecture management in a uniform manner for the topics of data, processes, and IT systems and translated into concrete actions and task packages within a joint implementation plan/transformation plan.

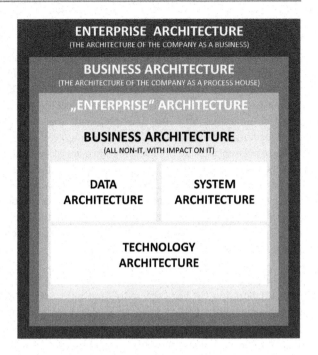

In order to leverage the benefits outlined for a company from the joint cooperation of processes, data, and IT systems, the cooperation of the three areas must be coordinated along the business architecture. The introduction of business architecture management has proven useful for this purpose.

Business architecture management is not a control unit in the sense of the change management task that has already been mentioned several times, but a forum that relies on voluntary participation. This means that business architecture management must repeatedly demonstrate the value of the close exchange of processes, data, and IT. This is most effectively achieved along two core themes for business architecture management: (1) common goals and (2) common tools and methods.

1. **Common goals:** Business architecture management as a forum for the three areas of "processes, data, and IT" creates a space for agreeing on goals. This does not mean that common goals are specified. The common goals meaningfully come further and solely from the hierarchically superior structures, such as the business or division management. In the common exchange room/forum of business architecture management, the individual units coordinate to jointly operationalize the higher level goals. This means that focal points for collaboration are developed and these are transferred into implementation plans at the working level. It is particularly valuable for the company if the three units have a shared and unified view of the challenges ahead and can thus also work independently in the coordinated direction. This shared view becomes even more valuable when it

comes to the joint cooperation projects, in which the units can thus work together in a more goal-oriented manner.

2. **Common tools and methods:** By aligning and jointly operationalizing the goals of the individual units from processes, data, and IT, a need for cooperation logically arises to solve these jointly identified tasks. During the initial collaboration between the units, it is usually noticeable that the individual professions differ fundamentally, for example, with regard to the way of working, the procedure, the methods, the technical language, and the departmental culture. If these peculiarities are not addressed in a coordinated manner, they lead at the very least to friction losses in productivity and, in the worst case, to competing units that work uncontrollably against each other instead of with each other. The easiest way to overcome these difficulties is to develop a common toolbox of methods and process models to accomplish the common tasks. This creates space for cooperation and at the same time leaves room for differentiation and for preserving one's own identity and culture.

While the previous chapters have discussed the groundwork for deep integration and collaboration between the individual units and, in particular, the role of Data Governance within the line and matrix organization in achieving this integration, the following chapters will focus on operationalizing the digital transformation using shared methods and common process models.

References

Bente S (2012) Collaborative enterprise architecture: enriching EA with Lean, Agile, and Enterprise 2.0 practices. Morgan Kaufmann, Burlington

Hadaya P, Gagnon B (2017) Business architecture: the missing link in strategy formulation, implementation and execution. ASATE Publishing, Montreal

Kotusev S (2018) The practice of enterprise architecture: a modern approach to business and IT alignment. SK Publishing, Melbourne

Yildiz M (2019) Agile business architecture for digital transformation: architectural leadership for competitive business value. S.T.E.P.S. Publishing, Roxburgh Park

Data Governance as Driver of Value Stream Optimization and as Pacemaker for the Digital Transformation

6

Abstract

Once you have found the right perspective on digital transformation, you realize that in addition to cultural "change," it is often just a matter of operationalizing solid craftsmanship (process models, methods, skills) for planning and implementing successful digital advancement. In other words, a company must begin to recognize digital transformation for what it has long been: a task that must be approached in a professional and structured manner. This task involves the company empowering its employees via specialist and methodological knowledge to be able to tackle the challenges of digitalization in a structured and collaborative manner. In this chapter, we will discuss this operationalization of digital transformation on the basis of a simple yet effective method, data-driven value stream optimization. Data-driven value stream optimization offers a clearly structured procedure for identifying digital development potential. By the end of this chapter, you will not only have a clear idea of the practical design of digital transformation options in your company's day-to-day operations, but will also be able to identify and implement them in a structured and methodical manner.

The method of digital value stream optimization builds on many of the fundamentals of classic value stream analysis familiar from the automotive industry. The classic value stream analysis only considers three basic dimensions for process optimization with time, material, and information flow (Martin 2013). It is precisely this simple view that has been successful and effective for decades in the manufacturing industry—and of course in many industries beyond. For modern, service-oriented companies with a high level of IT penetration, however, the classic value stream analysis offers too few starting points for identifying the relevant digital development potential.

By expanding the dimensions to be considered (from 3 to 8 dimensions) in the data-driven value stream analysis and a much stronger focus on the digital

© Springer-Verlag GmbH Germany, part of Springer Nature 2022
L. M. Bollweg, *Data Governance for Managers*, Management for Professionals,
https://doi.org/10.1007/978-3-662-65171-1_6

information flows (e.g., the exchange of data between systems and databases) and system functionalities (UX, system functions, etc.), manufacturing and service-oriented companies are enabled to identify digital potential along the business processes and to translate it into concrete IT requirements.

For a better understanding of data-driven value stream optimization, the basics of process documentation and the fundamentals of classic value stream analysis are first repeated. Only then will the methodological approach of data-driven value stream optimization be examined in greater depth and supplemented with examples of the concrete application of the method as a tool for identifying digital development potential in the context of digital transformation.

6.1   Fundamentals of Process Documentation

Many companies are practiced in mapping the activities and events along their processes in process flow diagrams. Today, professional notation languages such as UML or BPMN are already frequently used and thus create a clear view of the processes in the company. Far too often, these process documentations are oriented solely to the physical process chains. The perspective on data and systems is missing completely, partially, or only in an abbreviated form. In this context, the documentation of processes in the context of digital transformation usually fails not because of the recording of the respective digital facts, e.g., which data is used in which system, but often rather because of a clear, temporal classification of the documentation form. This means that, especially in the dynamic web of processes, data, and IT systems, it is not clear which status and which perspective the documentation produced reflects. For this reason, it is important to emphasize the temporal dimensionality of the process documentation in advance, as this will later be decisive for the design of data-driven value stream optimization discussed in the following chapters.

In process documentation, one classically considers one of three forms of documentation: (1) the ACTUAL documentation, (2) the IDEAL documentation, and (3) the TARGET documentation. Each of these forms of documentation can have an emphasis, a focus on all conceivable process dimensions, such as activities, data, and systems. So it is possible to document an ACTUAL, an IDEAL, and a TARGET process by also recording an ACTUAL, an IDEAL, or a TARGET IT architecture. The same is possible for the topic of data, i.e., process documentation focusing on the ACTUAL, IDEAL, or TARGET data process or data model (see Fig. 6.1).

Even though the emphasis and focus of a documentation can and in many use cases should change, it is important for successful process work to maintain an overview of the form of documentation used in each case. The basis for this is, of course, that one can clearly describe the distinction between ACTUAL, IDEAL, and TARGET and thus also clearly derive the consequences of the potentials found in the documentation.

Fig. 6.1 The temporal dimensions of process documentation © Lars Michael Bollweg 2022. All Rights Reserved

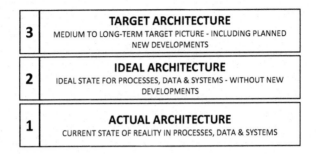

(1) **ACTUAL documentation:** The ACTUAL documentation describes the unadorned state of reality of a process and each of its dimensions (activities, data, systems, etc.). This form of documentation serves as the development basis for process optimization. It therefore describes what really is, without any planning intervention. In other words, the ACTUAL documentation is the starting point for every subsequent development and the final yardstick for process optimization success.

(2) **IDEAL documentation:** The IDEAL documentation, on the other hand, no longer describes reality and is already a first level of abstraction for the process as well as all its dimensions. The IDEAL documentation describes an idealized flow along a process with given means. The reference to the "given means" is important. An IDEAL process is an optimized version of the ACTUAL process, without the design elements (e.g., databases and system) having been changed compared to the ACTUAL documentation. Only the processes, i.e., the activities around the design elements, are optimized in the IDEAL documentation. The IDEAL documentation creates the basis for the control and planning optimization of the current process flows. It is the correction level for measuring the deviation of reality from the ideal.

(3) **TARGET documentation:** TARGET documentation is another abstraction form of ACTUAL and IDEAL documentation. It describes the optimal process with modified means. This means that in the TARGET documentation, creative means (e.g., new IT systems) are already deliberately included that are not yet available to the ACTUAL process. TARGET documentation is always a future perspective and, by looking ahead, provides the basis for the strategic further development of a process. Many process organizations neglect to maintain a TARGET process because they are afraid of the additional effort involved. This is understandable, but it leads to a blurring of IDEAL and TARGET documentation and many organizations simply lack an unbiased view of the future.

Each of the three forms of documentation thus has its own mission and its own application space. The ACTUAL documentation is the basis and starting point for the process work. The IDEAL documentation is the tool for controlling or operationally optimizing a process. The TARGET documentation is the basis for structured further development. If one wants to design a process successfully, each of the documentation forms should be used and mastered. Accordingly, each form of documentation can also be the basis for value stream optimization. And in the case of process work, each form of documentation is also part of value stream optimization at a certain point in time in the course of a process optimization measure. Because only with a structured view of what "ACTUAL" is can a meaningful "IDEAL" be developed and thus the process controlled. And only when "ACTUAL" and "IDEAL" are known can an innovative "TARGET" be targeted, toward which "ACTUAL" and "IDEAL" are aligned. This means that companies which are only concerned with the "IDEAL" may lose sight of the "ACTUAL" status and inevitably encounter difficulties in planning the "TARGET." And even worse: companies that present ACTUAL, IDEAL, and TARGET documentation at the same time and within a process map without consciously separating the forms of documentation usually have such a fuzzy level of abstraction that they are no longer able to make good decisions.

It is therefore advisable to have all forms of documentation available. However, this is an ideal state that one must also be able to afford. In the reality of finite resources, an IDEAL process is usually developed and continuously documented. This should be supplemented selectively by updated ACTUAL documentation in order to be able to derive control measures. A TARGET process is also frequently used in the same form. This is maintained selectively along modernization measures and is rarely considered in the overall context. Both compromises are understandable, but go hand in hand with limitations for the control and intervention options for process development. Only a view of all forms of documentation (ACTUAL, IDEAL, and TARGET) opens up an unobstructed view of the existing development potential of a process as a whole.

6.2　Classic Value Stream Mapping

The classic value stream mapping is an established method from the automotive industry. It has the charm that the identification of potentials for process optimization can be achieved with little means, e.g., even with a sheet of paper and a pencil. The classic value stream analysis is characterized by the fact that it combines value creation processes, e.g., three necessary processes for the creation of a product, into a common "value stream" (often End2End) at a very high flight level and identifies process potentials without much detail (Erlach 2020). The (internal or external) customer perspective is decisive for evaluating the success of a value stream. This means that at the end of a value stream there must always be a customer who evaluates the quality of the value stream, e.g., product quality or delivery time.

In the doctrine of classical value stream mapping, each value stream consists in its basic structure of individual processes (Martin 2013). Each process can be detailed again by event-driven process chains (EPC) or simple operation chains (OC) (see Fig. 6.2):

The classic value stream analysis usually remains on the surface of the value stream and only looks at the underlying processes from a distance. Value stream

Fig. 6.2 Overview of value stream, process, EPC, and OC © Lars Michael Bollweg 2022. All Rights Reserved

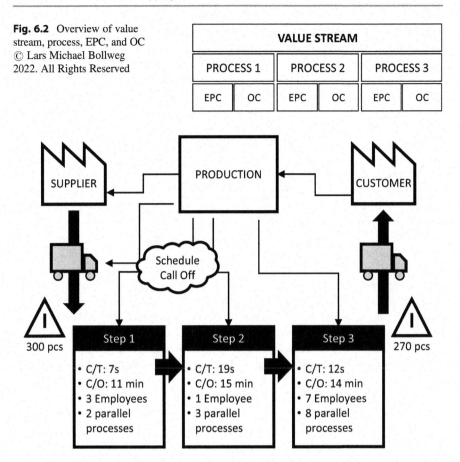

Fig. 6.3 Sketch of classic value stream analysis/value stream mapping © Lars Michael Bollweg 2022. All Rights Reserved

analysis abstracts the major lines into three dimensions: (1) the time stream, (2) the material stream, and (3) the information stream (see Fig. 6.3).

By focusing on the value stream along the lines of time, material, and information and, in particular, their interactions, the method makes it possible to easily identify optimization potential. These optimization potentials are structured along a group of optimization characteristics consisting of quality, efficiency, speed, and variability. These characteristics are interrelated, interdependent, and partially contradictory. This means, for example, that a process optimization in the direction of one of the characteristics influences the expression of another characteristic, i.e., improvement of quality is usually at the expense of speed in the process.

It is important to understand that the classic value stream mapping does not provide any concrete options for action from the methodology itself, but rather shows an optimization space that business experts must fill with the help of measures to be developed independently. Even though the methodology remains unspecific in its description of optimization potential, it does become very concrete in its evaluation of ACTUAL activities and their activity types.

In order to pay attention to the improvement of the desired optimization characteristics, classical value stream optimization identifies three different types of activities within the value streams: (1) useful activities (real value-adding work), (2) dummy activities (ancillary activities with a low value-added contribution), and (3) idle activities (wasted activities that do not generate any value added).

This results in two central application scenarios for the practical use of value stream mapping: (1) A company aims to use the results of value stream mapping to identify weaknesses in the value stream under consideration and to eliminate idle capacity and other process-related waste along the value stream. (2) The company tries to make the processes more efficient and effective by optimizing the time, material, and information flows.

As a result of a value stream mapping, concrete options for action emerge for the implementation of process improvements along the value stream. However, the concrete options for action are generated solely by the participants in the value stream mapping and are not supported by the method itself. In addition, the classic value stream mapping method is limited in its view of the process, and thus in its options, by the small number of process dimensions. Therefore, the method itself has few on-board resources of its own to get into a regular analysis of the value streams and a continuous improvement process with it. For this, the method is always dependent on external input, i.e., on the knowledge and creativity of the users and participants.

Despite the existing limitations, the value of classic value stream mapping for the optimization and further development of processes and workflows has been great in the past, especially for production-related companies. This is evidenced not only by the amount of literature on value stream mapping, but also by the high number of successful applications of this method in industry.

Unfortunately, value stream mapping has been somewhat overtaken by time, and the consideration of time, material, and information streams is no longer sufficient to deal with the increasingly complex reality of modern production and service companies. For many years, employees were still able to recognize the limited optimization options from their specialist knowledge alone and to derive the necessary action measures. But the ever-increasing challenges posed by the digital transformation in recent decades alone, such as the constant increase in automation levels to boost productivity in manufacturing and manufacturing-related companies, are pushing the traditional approach to the limit in terms of performance. Today, an employee would have to be a production specialist and data and IT expert all in one in order to independently overview all the necessary interrelationships and comprehensively identify their possible optimization potential. For classic value stream mapping, this means that the approach lacks the necessary digital perspective to guide users and employees in companies along the digital infrastructures to the often still untapped potential of digital transformation in a targeted and supportive manner. In other words, the weak point of classic value stream mapping is that it relies too heavily on a high level of technical and expert knowledge among the users of the method and that too little impetus for digitalization can be generated from the method itself.

Since this is a critical statement that is certainly worthy of discussion, it seems sensible to elaborate on this point further. It is true that it is right and important for a method to give users the greatest possible leeway in identifying courses of action— because the user usually knows better what will help the company than the method itself. But especially with regard to the options for action in the context of digital transformation, many employees lack the experience from their work history to be able to generate the necessary digital impulses themselves. In other words, it is often precisely the lack of expertise with regard to the potential of digital transformation (in the interaction of processes, data, and IT systems) that must be overcome as a development barrier with the help of such a method. Accordingly, it is important to maintain degrees of freedom in the run-through of a method, but at the same time it is necessary to make the solution spaces visible in order to bring the users of the method closer to their options for action, to inspire them, and to lead them to the goal.

This is where data-driven value stream optimization comes in. It offers tradition-ally organized companies in particular the necessary content-related and structural support in identifying digital development options and the basis for developing a clear roadmap in the direction of "digital transformation." Data-driven value stream optimization achieves its greatest effect in the context of coordinated and harmonized collaboration between the areas of processes, data, and IT in the sense of the business architecture management already introduced.

6.3 Data-Driven Value Stream Optimization

In addition to the professional management of data, i.e., the control, creation, use, maintenance, and further development of the data inventory within a company, the value of Data Governance lies in particular in the implementation of direct solutions and added value for the existing organization via the logic already introduced for the accompanying data projects. Particularly with a view to the future digital develop-ment of a company, Data Governance that is anchored in the process organization can make major contributions, e.g., development impulses and digital potential identification. Companies that also want to develop this transformational maturity level of Data Governance and use Data Governance as a driver of their own development are generally faced with two challenges: (1) How are the right and important data projects identified with regard to digital transformation? (2) How are these data projects prioritized and in what order are they implemented? To solve both challenges, data-driven value stream optimization can be helpful as a method and as a process model.

Principle 29: Data-driven value stream optimization helps companies identify digital development potential.

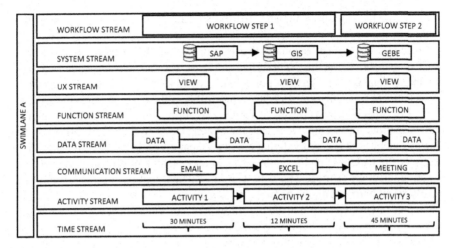

Fig. 6.4 Dimensions of data-driven value stream optimization © Lars Michael Bollweg 2022. All Rights Reserved

In the previous chapter, it was shown that data-driven value stream optimization is a further development of classic value stream analysis (value stream mapping), which in the past has become established primarily in the manufacturing industry. A value stream in the sense of classic value stream analysis is usually an End2End value creation process within a company, at the end of which there is a customer as the service recipient. In many companies, these processes are defined as core processes and part of the matrix organization, as they overlap the lines of the organizational structure.

Data-driven value stream optimization follows on from the logic of classic value stream analysis, but develops it further. Today, a large number of modern companies are no longer production companies in the classic sense, but are increasingly creating value through IT-supported service processes (Kersten 2019). This is the case, for example, when companies have outsourced their production or perform production themselves in a partially or fully automated manner along modern production lines. And finally, of course, also when a company does not produce at all and really operates on the market as a pure service provider.

For all these types of companies, classic value stream mapping does not offer any structural support in working out further development potential within the framework of digital transformation and has thus found its application limits. The pure focus on time, material, and information flows no longer sufficiently helps these IT and service-oriented companies to optimize their value creation processes.

To support these companies, it is necessary to re-tailor the classic dimensions of value stream mapping and enrich them with the logic of increasingly interconnected IT landscapes (Pilorget 2018). The result is a modern representation of the analysis and optimization of data-driven value streams that is flexible in its level of detail and geared toward service companies, with the goal of identifying digital development potential and its scope for implementation (see Fig. 6.4).

Data-driven value stream optimization looks at eight process dimensions. Each of the dimensions represents a further development space for the value stream in the context of digital transformation: (1) time stream, (2) activity stream, (3) communication stream, (4) data stream, (5) function stream, (6) user interface stream, (7) system stream, and (8) workflow stream.

Before we go into the application of the method and the appropriate procedure for its application, we explain each of the eight dimensions in brief. Within the following discussion of the relationships and dependencies between the process dimensions, these will also be deepened again.

(1) **Time stream:** In the time stream, the throughput times/running times of the individual activities are documented. The time that must be spent in order to perform a service is also decisive for measuring productivity in the digital age. High time contingents along a process activity point as an indicator to possible optimization potential (e.g., waste) along the other process dimensions (e.g., problematic functionalities) and are thus frequent starting points for a process analysis.

(2) **Activity stream:** The individual activities and events along the physical process steps are documented in the activity stream. The activity stream is the "main stream" in data-driven value stream optimization and sets the pace for all other streams. This means that the design of the activity stream (granularity of the activities) dictates the design of the entire process documentation (granularity of all other dimensions). If one details the activities, one gets a very detailed view of the process. If you aggregate the activities, you get a very simplified view of the process. It is important to recognize the activity stream as a control tool for process optimization. If the goal is to make very small-scale optimizations, detailing is helpful and necessary. If one wants to initiate rather large and overarching changes, an aggregated view is the better choice.

(3) **Communication stream:** All physical and digital information flows that are not automated via systems and databases are documented in the communication stream. Accordingly, in addition to physical meetings, telephone calls and personal conversations (verbal communication), and emails and letters (written communication), the communication stream also includes the content of physical and digital documents (unstructured data), insofar as these are used as a means of communication and information exchange. Example: If an Excel spreadsheet with information as an attachment is forwarded by email from one employee to the next in order to complete an important process step, then in this case this Excel file is also part of the communication stream and must therefore also be documented. The importance of the communication stream is often underestimated, but it is precisely this stream that has the potential to reveal so-called media discontinuities. A media break occurs when communication changes from one medium (e.g., email) to another (e.g., meeting) during the process. This change points to a variety of optimization points, among others automation potentials through digital communication flows or potentials for decision support systems such as early warning systems and dashboards and

many more. Especially the analysis of the communication flow in interaction with other dimensions such as the data flow or the UX flow often reveals great optimization potential for the process.

(4) **Data stream:** All information flows via databases (SQL and NoSQL) and interfaces (XML, JSON, etc.) are mapped in the data stream. The data stream is the turf of the digital process. It shows which information is generated, used, maintained, and deleted at which point in the process. The data stream thus forms the basis for the exchange of information between the IT systems and also the basis for the exchange of information between the IT systems and the users. To optimize the digital infrastructures of a process, a deep understanding of the data flows is crucial. A perfectly modeled data flow lays the foundation for an optimized IT landscape. Modern companies therefore no longer orient their process development on the functions of the applications and IT systems, but optimize these very IT systems "data-driven" along the information flows. Documenting the data flow is usually the biggest challenge for process teams. As with all process documentation challenges, complexity reduction is the biggest goal when documenting the data stream. Detailing the data stream is done when the data itself needs to be optimized. Until then, simplified data models (conceptual and logical data models) on a data object and data relationship level (e.g., entity-relationship modeling) can be used successfully. For the deep detailing of the physical data model and the data flows through the model, the framework of data-driven value stream optimization is usually left and a separate form of documentation is developed.

(5) **Function stream:** The function stream describes the individual system functionalities that must be executed to fulfill the process activities. This means that the capabilities of the systems are documented along the function stream, and at the same time, their shortcomings are also documented. Modeling the functional stream often makes IT development potentials most tangible, since the dimension of the systems is easiest for most employees to comprehend. It is easy to understand that to improve the process related to a unique activity, the functionality of the associated system must be improved. For the optimization of functions, the lower the level of abstraction of the system functions, in other words, the better the functional requirements are described, the easier it is to implement the necessary further development.

(6) **UX stream:** The UX stream describes the user interface, i.e., the visual representation of the system functionality with which the user interacts. The UX stream includes the complete human–computer interface—usually system dialogs and forms. In addition to the bare function, it is often the user interface that determines success or failure in optimizing a digital process. Are the work steps clear and intuitive for the user? Does the user interface support the creation and maintenance of information or is it rather a hindrance? Are forms pre-filled and input validated? Are texts and buttons large enough for users to work with effectively? The optimization potential of good user interfaces is enormous, and especially considering the operational reality, where user dialogs often still seem like underdeveloped relics from long ago, the fruit hangs deep here. A simple

question often already helps in identifying potential for improvement: Could we imagine the user dialog as an app on our private smartphone or would we rather opt for a more modern variant in the app store?

(7) **System stream:** The system stream or application stream documents the IT systems used within the process. The system stream shows in which system the respective activity is implemented with its data, functions, and user interface. In addition to the great optimization potential in the further development and merging of systems, the system stream also always acts as an orientation aid. The view of the system anchors the implementation potentials. These are always located within the system under consideration, within a replacement system to be redesigned, or between two systems. If it is determined during the optimization of the system stream that not only the level of the IT applications themselves is of importance, this stream can also be deepened to include the IT infrastructure (e.g., server—cloud vs. on premise). This is often the case when the optimization potential is found at the level of performance increases (e.g., availability and response times) and thus not at the functional or user interface dimension.

(8) **Workflow stream:** The workflow stream is the clock generator of digital workspaces. It creates a categorical bracket around the individual activities, communications, data, functions, user interfaces, and systems.

Within a workflow step, it is shown which activities can sensibly be carried out one after the other and often by the same employees within an operation and when this sensible connection ends. Workflow steps therefore create a further orientation and standardization perspective in order to structure the overall process more stringently and to optimize it in a more targeted manner. Buzzwords such as data, system, and process harmonization are important in this context.

A digital workflow with digital feedback points along a mainly manual process also creates the possibility of generating work statuses and evaluations along the course of the process, which is otherwise invisible to the digital systems, thus creating process transparency. The use of the workflow dimension is optional within data-driven value stream optimization. However, the use and, if necessary, the introduction of this process dimension is highly recommended.

Consideration of the eight process dimensions presented provides a complete view of the process optimization potentials of digital transformation. However, these potentials do not result from consideration of the dimensions alone, but also from consideration of the interactions and relationships of these dimensions and the granularity of the process modeling. Therefore, following the discussion of the individual process dimensions, it is important to also delve into the interdependencies of the eight process dimensions and the influence of the granularity of the process modeling. The procedure for process modeling is conceivably simple and will be taken up again in the following chapter on the application of the method. Before this, however, the basic orientation points for modeling a process and the associated process dimensions will be summarized once again in order to

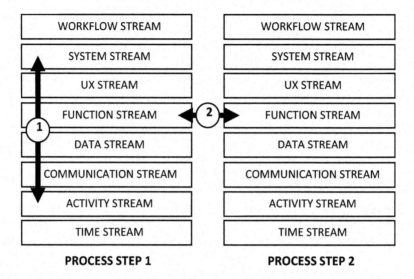

Fig. 6.5 Vertical and horizontal process optimization potentials © Lars Michael Bollweg 2022. All Rights Reserved

capture the process as purposefully as possible with the help of data-driven value stream optimization.

1. The documentation level (ACTUAL, IDEAL, TARGET) is clearly defined.
2. The activity stream is the structuring dimension for process modeling.
3. An activity can only represent one system at a time (largest granularity—upper limit).
4. It makes sense to start with the greatest possible granularity and to deal with the respective details along the process and identified potentials.
5. If the goal is to optimize user interfaces, functions, or data flows, it is necessary to further detail the granularity of the activities. As an example for the optimization of the user interface, an activity may only represent one interaction with one view of the user interface. The same procedure must be applied to functions and data.
6. By controlling the granularity, one controls the depth of optimization of the individual process dimensions.

To identify development potentials in the context of digital transformation, the individually recorded activities are enriched with information about the other dimensions of data-driven value stream optimization when modeling the value stream. The reciprocal relationships of the dimensions within an activity (vertical potentials) and the reciprocal relationships between activities (horizontal potentials) then provide a clear view of the overall digital development potentials in the process (see Fig. 6.5).

(1) **Vertical potentials:** Vertical potentials comprise all potentials that result from the alignment of the eight process dimensions along an activity. A few examples are (1) the absence of a function in the system to automate the activity, (2) the

optimization of the user interface with the help of new design elements (e.g., systems), or (3) also the improvement of the data situation by adding further attributes to a data object. Vertical potentials are so-called point potentials because they arise without considering the process and relate solely to the optimization of the individual activity. However, these optimization potentials must not be underestimated in terms of value, since the optimization of the points in the process naturally also improves the entire process.

(2) **Horizontal potentials:** Horizontal potentials comprise all optimization potentials resulting from the comparison of the eight process dimensions of an activity with the eight process dimensions of the predecessor and successor activities. Examples include interface and functional potentials for automating information flows in databases and systems. However, the planning and development of completely new IT systems with disruptive effects on the overall process can also result from the horizontal or also process-related consideration of the development potential.

By looking at the intersections of the process dimensions along the activity (vertical) and along the process (horizontal), the basis for data-driven value stream optimization has already been created. Like classic value stream optimization, from this point on users could already identify optimization measures based on their own knowledge and transfer them to implementation. However, data-driven value stream optimization even supports the user group with defined process optimization categories, which are intended to accelerate the development of options for action as orientation, inspiration, and driving force.

Process Optimization Categories
Like traditional value stream mapping, data-driven value stream mapping leaves a lot of room (degrees of freedom) for developing innovative solutions along the value stream. But unlike the traditional approach, data-driven value stream optimization supports optimization with eight optimization categories along the eight process dimensions presented. Each optimization category can be held like a focus topic against the created process documentation, thus visualizing the space of possibilities for the user group of the method. In other words, it is never necessary, nor is it ever purposeful, to consider and optimize all dimensions simultaneously within a workshop. It may well make sense to define a focus for the optimization measures in advance, and the following optimization categories of data-driven value stream mapping will help with this:

1. Process and workflow optimization
2. Communication optimization
3. Data and dataflow optimization
4. Interface and interoperability optimization
5. System function optimization
6. UX optimization

7. Full system development
8. Workflow optimization

Each of the eight optimization categories leads the user group to a large number of development potentials. To ensure that a company does not collapse under the flood of possible development potentials, it is important to evaluate each identified development potential also under the consideration of the optimization characteristics: quality, economic efficiency, speed, and variability which are also used for the classic value stream analysis, and to establish a prioritization on this basis.

Caution: A targeted process and system optimization must not be viewed only one-dimensionally from the direction of efficiency gains for the existing processes and systems. Of course, automation is the ultimate goal of process optimization. And of course automation saves human labor. But if saving manpower is the only value a company can generate through digitalization, then the company is falling far short of its existing capabilities. It's true that every company needs to save money, so it wants to shorten lead times, eliminate procedural bottlenecks, and generally reduce procedural costs. But a company should also always look for ways to generate new and innovative added value with the help of digitalization, for example, producing more, providing more services (productivity increase), producing differently, if necessary digitally, and providing other services (innovation, disruption): in other words—to become better with the help of digitalization—not just cheaper.

Data-driven value stream optimization offers companies the opportunity to operationalize the further development of the company's own processes and systems via a structured method. And if innovation and further development are part of a company's standard toolbox, then digitalization loses its abstract character and can be planned and implemented in the company via tangible and clear measures. And that is why data-driven value stream optimization also offers companies the optimal basis for a controlled development of their own digital transformation.

The fact that all the basics of data-driven value stream mapping have already been covered at this point once again highlights the impressive simplicity and self-explanatory logic of the method. In the following section, the knowledge gained in this chapter will be built upon once again and the concrete procedure, i.e., the actual application of the method, will be further deepened and the theory discussed will be transferred into practice.

6.4   Application of Data-Driven Value Stream Optimization

The greatest challenge to the successful use of structured methods for process optimization is the transfer of theory into practice. Many methods sound good on paper, but have a multitude of complex rules and struggle with limitations in practical application. Data-driven value stream optimization, on the other hand, is as simple in application as the application of classic value stream analysis has always been. The simple and structured process of data-driven value stream optimization therefore also fits smoothly into the toolbox of established process work, which is why the method is easy to adapt and use, even for inexperienced teams. You could do it with just a piece of paper and a pencil and already achieve value-added results for the company. Fortunately, however, process optimization methods no longer have to be implemented with just pencil and paper. The use of interactive and group-friendly tools (offline: flipcharts and post-its, online: digital whiteboards and other cooperation and collaboration tools) not only has a positive impact on the commitment of the employees involved, but also helps to keep track of a possible flood of identified optimization potential.

However, as with the use of any method, both preparation and practical implementation are critical to success. For this reason, all the necessary components of good planning and preparation are discussed below, followed by a further in-depth look at practical implementation.

Preparation
Good preparation when using a method consists of a number of critical elements. Among the most important are (1) clear goal planning, (2) identification of a suitable value stream, (3) determination of the implementation format as well as the group of participants, and (4) final time and process planning.

In the following, the method and detailed procedure for using data-driven value stream optimization are presented along the four categories mentioned.

Target Planning
Data-driven value stream optimization is a method for identifying development potentials in the context of digital transformation (e.g., identification of process and workflow potentials, data and data flow potentials, and system and workflow potentials). This means that the use of the method is suitable whenever companies are looking for digital value creation potential or digitally enabled efficiency potential along a process chain (e.g., digitally enabled automation and system optimization in the sense of new and further developments). Since the space of possibilities is large and the complexity of the individual dimensions is high, it is helpful for successful implementation of the method to commit in advance to a defined target corridor for the desired optimization measures and not to search globally for potentials of all optimization categories at once. The cornerstones for a meaningful target corridor usually consist of decisions on (1) the documentation form, (2) the digital target value-added stage, and the (3) optimization category or categories.

Form of Documentation The most fundamental decision in the planning of a data-driven value stream optimization is the decision for the form of documentation: ACTUAL, IDEAL, or TARGET documentation. This decision forms the basis for the location of the targeted optimization measures and the resulting consequences. Measures that are based on the ACTUAL documentation can usually be implemented directly, while any dependencies on process models that have not yet been implemented in everyday life must be taken into account from the IDEAL documentation level of abstraction. The number of such dependencies increases again immensely in the context of TARGET documentation, since some process components, often IT systems, have not yet reached the employee. Despite existing challenges, IDEAL documentation is the standard form of documentation because it is already oriented to the idealized process flow and thus develops the process to the highest level of optimization. Only if the documented TARGET process is fundamentally divergent from the reality of the ACTUAL process, i.e., the TARGET has little to do with reality, is it more promising to build on the ACTUAL process and thus completely redevelop the IDEAL and TARGET process. A sense of proportion is therefore necessary in the preparation, and a realistic self-assessment is helpful.

Digital Target Value Creation Stage It can also be helpful to consider the desired goal along the digital value creation stages before starting the optimization measure. Although many companies often proclaim "automation" as the top goal, it is nevertheless valuable to consider the other digital value creation stages as well. A look at the entire range of possibilities makes it possible to identify value-creating digitalization measures even at those points where automation is not easy to achieve, e.g., with partial automation.

Optimization Categories The decision before performing a data-driven value stream mapping for a focus, i.e., for a limited look at one of the eight optimization categories, is optional and remains reserved for the user group of the method. However, it is easy to get lost in the details of the individual process dimensions, especially in long process chains. Therefore, it is not wrong to go into the application of data-driven value stream mapping with knowledge of all optimization categories, but with a clear focus on only one or two of the optimization categories in the workshop.

Furthermore, it is helpful to use this focus to control the granularity of process modeling in a targeted manner. This means that a clear focus in advance helps to avoid unnecessary documentation efforts and to effectively identify the desired optimization potentials through the application. If a prior focus is not possible for the user group because of, for example, too little existing process knowledge, it makes sense to start with a high aggregation level and then deepen the granularity in view of individual potentials.

Based on the target corridor, all subsequently required decisions for planning and preparation can be made in a targeted manner.

Format and Participant Group

Data-driven value stream optimization is most successful in developing and modeling the individual process and system potentials when employees from the business units (domain experts), the process teams (flow experts), the data teams (information flow experts), and the IT teams (system experts) work together. Therefore, it also makes sense to select a workshop format for conducting the data-driven value stream mapping. When it comes to conducting a workshop today, it makes little difference whether the workshop is organized online or offline; it is more important to bring the right people together in an open and creative environment. In addition to the subject matter experts for the ACTUAL state from the operational departments, it always makes sense to include one or two innovators in the group. An innovator is usually a person who critically questions the process and regularly develops new ideas for improvement. Fortunately, innovative personalities can be found in almost all companies. If this is not the case in the company, it is a good idea to call on outside help.

A group size of four to eight participants has proven to be ideal when working out the digitalization potential. If there is a clear focus on one optimization category, it also makes sense to include a subject matter expert for the respective category (e.g., interfaces and system functionalities) in the team. Of course, one person, i.e., one employee, can also be an expert for more than just one of the mentioned categories. If this is the case, the workshop benefits from this, as it is possible to work more efficiently in smaller groups.

Identification of a Suitable Value Stream
In contrast to the classic value stream analysis, the data-driven value stream analysis does not only aim at a high-level view of the overall process. As a method, data-driven value stream mapping can be applied to all process levels as long as there is an activity reference. The flexibility in examining the eight process dimensions (time, activities, communication, data flows, system functions, user interface, system, and workflow) also makes it easy to apply the method at process and operation chain level.

The selection of the right process scaling, the so-called granularity of observation, is therefore no longer limited by the method itself, as is the case with classic value stream mapping, but can be freely selected depending on requirements and the use case.

If the process is still at a low level of digitalization maturity, i.e., if few digital tools are in use and a low level of automation has generally been reached, it can make sense to start looking for optimization potential at a high altitude, e.g., as part of a roughly sketched End2End process. The higher-level view then makes it possible to illuminate the major optimization breakpoints (workflow, systems, interfaces) and to arrive at optimization potentials that are generally easy to depict. These are easy to find, but they are also usually investment intensive.

If a higher level of maturity of digitalization has already been reached in the process, i.e., many digital tools and a high degree of automation, it also makes sense to take a closer look at the deeper level of detail (UX, functions, data quality). This detailed view makes it possible to improve already highly optimized processes even further, e.g., through optimized user dialogs in the views of the individual systems or optimized data qualities for new system functions. These optimization measures are often less expensive to implement, but they rarely have a transformational, disruptive character; instead, they really only have an optimizing character.

Often, the scope of possibilities also dictates the scaling level and thus the granularity required. If one is tasked with scrutinizing a process as a whole and redesigning it with large development projects, a higher, less detailed approach is again helpful. However, if one is tasked with identifying efficiency measures in an existing system, starting at a more detailed level is the right place to start.

This means that to identify the right scaling level and thus the right value stream, you need a clear mission with an optimization target and a realistic view of the ACTUAL state of the current processes.

If this clear view exists, the selection of the right value stream follows on its heels. If I want to optimize the interface between systems, I need a value stream that spans these systems. If I want to optimize the activities for a specific activity type (e.g., contract data documentation), I need a value stream that spans these activities.

Always helpful is the reference to complexity reduction. Simplify the processes you want to optimize as often and as far as possible. Rather start small (low granularity) and add more information in the course of the optimization project (higher granularity) than drown in complexity from the beginning.

Implementation
To successfully apply the method, it is important to internalize not only the (1) general process for process modeling but also the (2) use of "perspective changes" (e.g., focus on the "data" dimension or on the "UX" dimension) along the process dimensions to identify development potential.

In the following, we will go into more detail about both the process of the method and the structured application of perspective shifts.

Procedure
The process of data-driven value stream optimization follows only a few basic rules:

(1) Data-driven value stream optimization always starts with an initial modeling of the activity stream. The activity stream is the clock generator of the method. It is therefore often referred to as the main stream. It is important to note that the entire process does not necessarily have to be considered in order to carry out the method. It can also be useful to start with only a self-contained subset, i.e., a sub-process. In practice, this means that existing process modeling at the OC or EPC level is an ideal starting point for using data-driven value stream optimization. This form of documentation forms a clear starting point from which the view of the process can be deepened in iterative steps.

(2) In the second step, the seven other dimensions of data-driven value stream optimization are documented for each activity along the activity stream. That is, a profile is created for each activity, which provides insights into the relationship of the activity to the other dimensions. How much time is required to complete the activity? What communication accompanies the activity? What system is involved? If the modeling of the process is done physically, it is suitable to develop a simple template on sticky notes for documenting each activity and its associated dimensions (example—see Figs. 6.6 and 6.7). If the modeling takes place in a digital framework, for example on a whiteboard or collaboration tool, it makes sense to design the dimensions on individual, clearly assignable levels. The process flow and the connection of the individual levels to

Fig. 6.6 Activity profile—
data-driven value stream
optimization © Lars Michael
Bollweg 2022. All Rights
Reserved

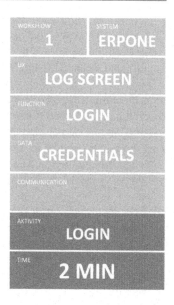

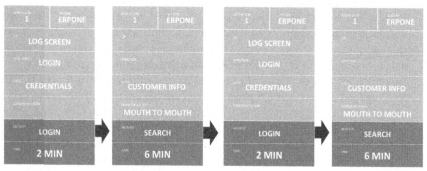

Fig. 6.7 Processual representation of data-driven value stream optimization © Lars Michael Bollweg 2022. All Rights Reserved

each other should remain visible. This approach helps to keep order when modeling the process so that the complexity of the documentation does not obscure the view of the process. In addition, it inevitably leads to compliance with the following basic rules.

- An activity can only include one system at a time.
- An activity can include multiple UX views, functional flows, data flows, and communication flows.
- Perspective change: If the goal is to optimize UX, functions, data, or communication, then an activity should also include only one UX view, function, data flow, or communication flow.

- Within each modeled activity, the eight optimization categories are examined (vertically) and potentials found are documented.
- Between all modeled activities the respective interfaces are examined (horizontally) and again the found potentials are documented.

Identification of Development Potential
By examining the dimensions of the individual process activities (vertical potentials) and the interfaces between the process activities (horizontal potentials) in the workshop, it is possible to identify development potentials for the process as well as for the data and for the IT systems. To do this, the user teams can follow one of two process models or combine them.

(1) **Free identification of development potentials:** As with classic value stream mapping, users of the method can be guided through the process and allowed to freely identify optimization potentials based on the types of activities presented within the value streams (useful activities—real value-added work, sham activities—ancillary activities with a low value-added contribution, and idle activities—wasted activities that do not generate any value added). Freely in this sense means free from specifications and thought structures. The users of the method are solely dependent on their own field of experience, but are not restricted in their creativity by specifications. This approach is valuable if the user group can overview all dimensions with their own capabilities and is thus able to recognize the digital potentials and translate them into requirements.

(2) **Identification of development potential along optimization categories:** The identification of development potential with the help of optimization categories builds on the experience that, particularly in traditional companies, the possibilities of digitalization are not yet integrated as standard knowledge in the experience of employees. Therefore, the optimization categories show the way to the users of the method. Along (1) process optimization, (2) communication optimization, (3) data and dataflow optimization, (4) interface and interoperability optimization, (5) system function optimization, (6) UX optimization, (7) full system development, and (8) workflow optimization, users can gradually shift their focus to individual topics in the workshop, discuss them, and identify possible optimization potential.

Regardless of which approach is chosen, the company usually has two lists of optimization potentials as a result of a workshop. The first list contains all vertical optimization potentials: in other words, all potential optimization measures that relate to only one activity. The second list contains all horizontal optimization potentials, i.e., all potential measures that cover one or more activities. Since not every identified development potential also has real implementation potential, it is necessary to pre-assess the potentials at the end of a workshop, for example, along the categories of feasibility (realistically realizable/not realizable) and potential/effort (effort—low, medium, high/impact—low, medium, high) to evaluate and, if necessary, also in a heat map to present.

At the end of the prioritization process, a prioritized and detailed requirements specification has emerged, which passes on the potential of digital transformation to the digital production line of IT development.

6.5   The Digital Production Line

The final stage in establishing Data Governance is to connect the data organization to the company's digital production line. If you look back at the contents of this book, you will see that up to this point an organizational structure has been developed that is not only capable of professionally managing the handling of data but also enables the company to identify innovative IT requirements and IT development potential at high speed and prepare them for implementation by looking at processes, data, and IT systems and using the right methods and tools.

Until the IT requirement is identified, prioritized, and defined, the supporting units of the line or matrix organization, e.g., process management, are the most active partners of Data Governance in the enterprise. This is where this book could end. However, if a flood of identified requirements and development potential gets bogged down at the interface with IT, the company has not taken a step forward. In fact, the opposite is true. Unmet requirements lead to frustration, resignation, and dissatisfaction in the company with the IT department. That's why it's important to think the digital development and exploitation chain through to the end: from the identification of the requirement to the acceptance of the requirement by the IT department to the final implementation. Because it is precisely at the interface between data-driven process and system optimization and digital further development, i.e., the acceptance of the requirement by IT, that the final challenge in digital transformation begins: the digital production line.

In view of the digital production line, the interaction of the partners also changes. Whereas up to now processes and data along the IT systems have been in intensive exchange (professional management of data, identification of potential, and development of requirements), from now on IT systems begin to exchange intensively with the processes about the implementation of IT (further) developments (requirements acceptance, requirements assessment, requirements specification, and final requirements development) along the digital production line (Stationary Office 2019). The exchange format for this close coordination between data and IT teams is the identified IT requirements from the processes, e.g., requirements for implementations of standard software, change requests, customizations, or requirements directly for completely new developments of applications and applications.

With the start of the digital production line, the units of IT, i.e., the classic IT departments (IT management) and the IT development departments (IT development), take on the active part. They are responsible for ensuring that identified and prioritized requirements are implemented as quickly as possible (time to market).

This change of role is particularly difficult for traditional companies that rely heavily on standard software to achieve their corporate goals and have not established their own development units within the company. Without major options for intervention and change in the existing IT landscape, the development of an efficient digital production line is often a costly and unsuccessful undertaking. The limited customization options of standard digital solutions act as a development barrier to digital transformation in traditional companies.

But even companies with an IT department capable of development face major challenges along the digital production line. The IT departments often take over requirements completely and forget to involve the business department as an internal customer in the development process at an early stage. This leads to the IT departments acting as the "owner" of the requirement and often making their assessment independently and detached from the existing needs of the business departments. This decoupling of IT from the real requirements of the business departments is particularly damaging because the inevitably resulting undesirable developments only become apparent after the investment in the development, i.e., during the implementation. This is also even more problematic because it reinforces the negative tendency for business processes to continue to adapt to the functions of the standard software, rather than the software optimally supporting the business processes.

For companies that want to increase their competitiveness through the use of digital technologies, this means that they should work purposefully on increasing the possible intervention and change options along the IT landscape in their software applications as well as on early and intensive business department involvement in ongoing IT developments. Both of these skills are fundamental prerequisites for avoiding reaching a dead end with IT development.

To purposefully circumvent this impasse, a company must recognize that a high degree of influence on the design of digital infrastructures is just as critical to success as influence on the design of physical processes. No successful manufacturing company would purchase equipment and machinery that it could not adapt to its own manufacturing processes. In exactly the same way, a company must also think about IT systems. However, it is not necessary for every company to develop every piece of software in the company itself. But it must be ensured that the software packages that map key company processes, such as ERP systems, have options for intervention and change in order to adapt to the company's needs.

For the purposeful development of a digital production line, a company, and in particular the IT department of a company, must logically develop efficient processes in four disciplines in order to serve the requests from the business department: (1) implementation request, (2) change requests, (3) customizing request, and (4) development request (see Fig. 6.8).

The development of these capabilities is not part of this book. The following chapter therefore serves as a source of inspiration and a guide for other topics that a company should master as part of the digital transformation. However, these are precisely the topics and challenges that should be realized subsequently or directly in step with the establishment and implementation of Data Governance so that a

MATURITY OF THE DIGITAL PRODUCTION LINE	
1	IMPLEMENTATION REQUEST
2	CHANGE REQUEST
3	CUSTOMIZING REQUEST
4	DEVELOPMENT REQUEST

Fig. 6.8 Maturity of the digital production line © Lars Michael Bollweg 2022. All Rights Reserved

company is able to realize the added value from the organizational development described in this book as quickly as possible. A final focus is then placed on dealing with requirements in the customizing process, since the ability to customize usually has the greatest intersection with responsive Data Governance as a driver of process and system development.

(1) Implementation Request The introduction of new software, i.e., software implementation, is a challenging but thoroughly familiar standard activity in many companies. Especially the so-called greenfield implementations, where one introduces a completely new software without existing legacy in the company, usually run more or less smoothly. Difficulties usually only arise here in the case of deviations from the tried and tested, familiar standard, for example, when you switch to a cloud environment for the first time after many years and broad experience with on-premise implementations. Or also when you implement your first in-house developments after a large number of implementations of standard software.

The challenges for IT departments become more difficult and more serious in the case of so-called brownfield implementations. These involve the replacement and renewal of existing systems while taking existing processes and data into account, i.e., taking legacy systems into account. These types of implementations usually entail extensive data migration processes. Large migration projects in particular often take IT organizations to their limits, which is why pragmatic solutions often have to be preferred to completely correct ones. But it is precisely pragmatism in data migrations that in many cases leads to years of data quality problems. These are often "invisible" at first and the resulting consequences often only become apparent to the company when the next stage of development is to be started, but the data and processes are not designed for this.

Despite all the existing challenges, the ability to implement and successfully implement the processes accompanying the implementation can be assumed as a standard capability in IT departments today.

(2) **Change Requests** The implementation of so-called "changes," i.e., the implementation of standard change requests (e.g., updates, patches, etc.) to existing systems, is just as much a standard activity of an IT organization today as implementation and operation. Change requests therefore also run hand in hand with the operation of a software or application under the term "maintenance." In summary, all the changes that are necessary for the long-term successful operation of the software are combined here. The broadness of the term "change request," however, allows a variety of interpretations as to what kind of requirements can be behind a concrete "change request." In practice, there are many variants in dealing with this topic. There are companies that deal with IT requirements in a differentiated manner, and there are companies that basically classify every system change as a "change request." For the purposes of this book, however, a "change request" is a change requirement that arises from the operation of the software itself and the associated legal framework. This excludes and delimits all requirements that are brought to IT from the business department for the further development of the digital capabilities of a software product. The requirements in this category are summarized below under the group of "Customizing Requests."

(3) **Customizing Request** Compared to the "Change Request," the challenge for a company becomes more complex with the "Customizing Request." This is not only because the company enters into much more intensive communication with the software developer during customizing (How can the software be adapted? What consequences does the adaptation have for other areas of the software?) than in the case of a simple "change," but above all because the company must assume joint responsibility for the product to be changed. In concrete terms, this means that by formulating and specifying the customizing requirements, a company itself helps to determine the outcome and scope of performance of the new system. It can then no longer place responsibility for the scope of performance solely with the software provider, but is an integral part and active driver of software development. This role, which is often new for companies, must be filled professionally; otherwise, the new tool will not ultimately fit the task in the company.

Strong customizing skills also enable traditional companies to free themselves from the shackles of standard software and adapt applications as optimally as possible to their own workflows and processes. Customizing is therefore an efficient way to shape a company's digital development without having to do any development yourself. A focus on customizing is accordingly a strategic decision that a company can choose on the journey toward "digital transformation." This stage can also be seen as an intermediate step to developing software yourself.

(4) **Development Requests** Developing software in-house, i.e., software development, naturally gives a company the greatest possible freedom in designing its own

processes and implementing innovative ideas. Only companies that are able to drive forward their own developments and implement them in their own digital products are in a position to effectively realize the maximum added value of the company's digital potential. But this sounds easier than it is. The development of software involves a great deal of effort (time, personnel, etc.) and the company always bears the potential risk of failing to meet the requirements of the company or the market with its own development.

An effective development unit within a traditional company can only be successfully mastered within the framework of a professional organization, usually agile, with a high level of involvement of the specialist department. Here, we come full circle with the challenges of cultural change management, which were already intensively discussed at the beginning of the book. Successful companies will be those that actively shape and develop their corporate culture in parallel with progressive digitalization and the transformation of corporate processes.

At the end of the digital transformation, every company is a software company. And every company will strategically develop processes and implement projects at all levels of digital capabilities (implementation, change, customizing, and development).

It is important that companies prepare for this today and implement strategic priorities in the individual areas step by step. For example, it is not necessary to develop or customize software directly yourself if standard software does the job perfectly. However, it can bring enormous efficiency gains if, for example, manual intervention by employees in information and decision flows is minimized by customizing system functions and data interfaces.

If these arguments are followed, it becomes apparent how strongly the maturity of a company's customizing capabilities will become a success factor in the context of digital transformation. Especially in the phase of transition from a traditional to a data-driven software company, customizing is a key competence. The Data Governance presented here in this book and the methods for identifying development potential pay to a large extent precisely to this adaptability of corporate IT, primarily, of course, with the delivery of development potentials. Therefore, to conclude this book, it makes sense to look again at exactly the interface between data-driven value stream optimization within the Data Governance work and the digital production line. This interface lies precisely between the identification of requirements by the business unit with the help of Data Governance and the acceptance of requirements by the IT organization.

The exchange format for this interface is the requirement itself, or requirements documentation. Target-oriented requirements documentation is part of a lean requirements management process. Such a requirements management process is needed between the identification of requirements in the business department and the implementation of the requirement by the company's own IT development or by an IT service provider. The efficiency of such a process is often measured by the key figure "time to market," i.e., the time that a requirement takes from identification and prioritization to implementation. However, the requirements process can only really influence the processes between requirements identification and the final handover of the requirement to IT development for implementation. For the last mile, the requirements process relies on the capabilities of the development processes in the company. From the identification of a requirement to its handover to development, the requirements process must evaluate, specify, and validate the requirement in multiple steps until a smooth transition to IT development can be ensured. This means that a requirement must also undergo a certain maturing and refining process in order to also be ready for implementation.

Three characteristics are crucial for the success of such a process: firstly, permanent requirement transparency vis-à-vis the business units and IT (status of the requirement), secondly, communication with the help of requirements documentation along the requirements process (evaluation, specification, and validation), and finally, the design of clear, formalized decision points to ensure a smooth refinement process of the requirement.

The design and optimization of the requirements process is not part of this book, but the interface to the requirements process, the requirements handover, is. Therefore, the design of the requirements documentation will be discussed at the end of this chapter. With the help of good requirements documentation, companies can complete the handover of development potential to IT in a targeted and efficient manner.

The goal of good requirements documentation must be to ensure that as many bases as possible for decisions related to assessment, specification, and validation are already collected by the requirements documentation so that the subsequent processes in IT can run through quickly and without major rework and costly loops. Target-oriented requirements documentation itself often consists of two elements: (1) requirements description, assessment, and specification (user stories, ACTUAL-IDEAL comparison, system development canvas, and assessment heat map) and (2) wireframing and rapid prototyping for requirements validation. With the delivery of the complete requirements documentation, the IT department is ready for development.

Requirements documentation is the natural connection point to the work within Data Governance. The approach to proactive Data Management presented in this book, with the goal of using process and system optimization as a digitalization driver, inevitably flushes a large number of optimization potentials to the edge of the IT organization. As a rule, there are far too many for the IT organization to convert all of them into developments and implement them at the same time. Inevitably, it is necessary to evaluate and prioritize in order to implement the most valuable potential for the company first. In order to be able to implement this evaluation in a targeted manner as part of a requirements management process, requirements documentation and the associated requirements document are the key to a smooth process flow. It makes sense to create the requirements documentation within the process organization, together with data and IT experts, in order to provide a realistic view of the requirement directly.

As a <user>...	I want <target>	so that / because <reason>
As a purchasing clerk...	I would like to have a digital invoice control....	so that I save time and deliver better quality of work.

Fig. 6.9 Example user story © Lars Michael Bollweg 2022. All Rights Reserved

(1) Requirements Description, Evaluation, and Specification The core of any further development is the translation of the business requirement into an artifact that can be implemented by the IT department. To do this, the requirement from the business unit must be described and evaluated in terms of its importance.

(a) User stories: Defining the requirements within so-called user stories has proven successful. User stories draw a large frame around the requirements and show which group in the company (Who?) has which requirement (What?) and what they want to achieve with it (What for?). Often, the creation of user stories alone will reveal whether or not the requirement is truly legitimate and significant. The creation of a user story always follows the same simple structure:

> *"As a <user>, I want <target> so that/because <reason>."*

Classically, user stories are recorded in table form in order to be able to compare them clearly (see Fig. 6.9).

(b) ACTUAL-IDEAL comparison, system landscape in the process: Once you have documented the project, it makes sense to outline the consequences of this requirement. A first step toward understanding the task at hand is an ACTUAL-IDEAL comparison along the affected systems. This means that at a very high level of fluency, it is written down for each system what the current status is in the system and what will change with the implementation of the requirement (see Fig. 6.10).

(c) System development canvas: Once the major changes have been outlined, it makes sense to then translate the measures to be implemented into clearly specified work packages; i.e., for each affected system, the individual changes to be implemented as a result of the requirement should be specified in detail and at various levels. In other words, the changes to be made to the user interface, functions, and databases should be recorded for each system so that the IT departments have a clear idea of the effort to be expected (see Fig. 6.11).

(d) Evaluation heat map: As a final valuable component of the requirements documentation, it makes sense to have the requesting department evaluate the requirement on an evaluation heat map along the dimensions of potential and effort or even importance and urgency. This evaluation is, of course, only the most rudimentary form of evaluation. For many companies with a large number of requirements, it may also make sense to require even more in-depth assessments as a filter for the requirements, e.g., the calculation of business cases, the use of

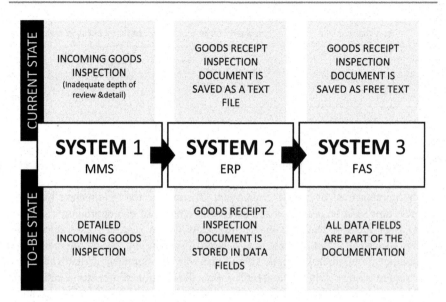

Fig. 6.10 ACTUAL-TARGET comparison of system landscape in process © Lars Michael Bollweg 2022. All Rights Reserved

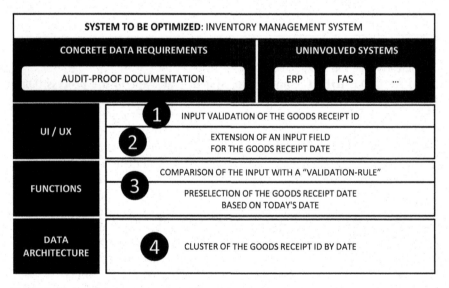

Fig. 6.11 System development canvas © Lars Michael Bollweg 2022. All Rights Reserved

scoring methods, or the performance of more in-depth analyses such as DMAGIC from Six Sigma. But in small and medium-sized companies, even simpler means are sufficient for assessing and prioritizing the vast majority of requirements (see Fig. 6.12).

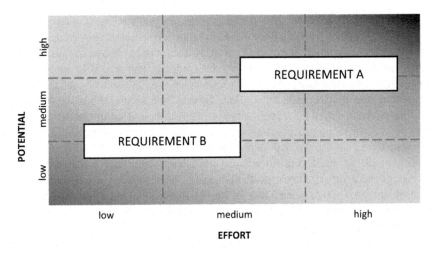

Fig. 6.12 Evaluation heat map © Lars Michael Bollweg 2022. All Rights Reserved

(2) Wireframing and Rapid Prototyping Based on the detailed and prioritized requirement it is possible to design a first prototype for the development. A fast and inexpensive prototype (rapid prototyping) serves on the one hand to visualize the planned changes in the systems, but also at the same time to validate the set requirements. So-called wireframes have established themselves in the area of rapid prototyping as both an effective and inexpensive solution. The term wireframe comes from architecture and stands for a miniature wire model of a building, i.e., a simplified representation of reality without any "supporting" substance or function. This is exactly how wireframes are used in digital development. They represent, for example, the computer–human interfaces, e.g., the user interfaces, via simple graphical illustrations, and thus enable a quick check of the planning against the users' expectations. The functions are only hinted at or, if necessary, re-enacted by changing a view, as in a flip book. The user must therefore bring a certain amount of imagination with him, but can already orient himself very strongly to the "wireframe" and give the developers feedback early in the development process. The use of wireframes not only makes development cheaper, as the need for subsequent correction loops is greatly reduced. They also lead to a very early involvement of users in the development and thus to a very high later acceptance of the solution in the company. The ability to quickly develop prototypes and test them before high development costs have been accumulated is another key skill along the digital production line.

Based on all these components of the requirements documentation, it is very quickly possible for companies to describe the development potential identified by the Data Governance work in the processes and make them ready for transfer to the digital production line.

By the end of this chapter, you should have understood that Data Governance can be a valuable building block within the digital transformation of your company. But it is only a building block. If you really want to anchor deep change and progressive digital and data-driven development in your company and lead it to success, you must understand Data Governance as a foundation, i.e., as the basis for the digital production line that is built on it. Data Governance secures your data and the handling of your data with a professional organization and, in interaction with the units around corporate processes and IT systems, develops the potential for optimization up to the handshake with digital development.

As part of the digital transformation, companies today face a number of new challenges and a variety of new skills that need to be introduced and developed. It is not problematic if you develop a little or step by step in all areas. The main thing is to start strengthening your organizational capabilities to continue to be successful in the future dominated by digital solutions.

A good point for getting started with implementing Data Governance can be found in the next and last chapter with the introduction of a maturity matrix and a short self-assessment questionnaire. After that, you will find all the principles we have highlighted in a common list again, as well as our conclusion, a glossary, and a bonus chapter on writing data definitions.

References

Stationary Office (2019) Itil Foundation: Itil4, 4th edn. Stationary Office Books, London

Kersten M (2019) Project to product: how to survive and thrive in the age of digital disruption with the flow framework. IT Revolution PR, Portland

Martin K (2013) Value stream mapping: how to visualize work and align leadership for organizational transformation. McGraw-Hill Education, New York

Pilorget L (2018) IT management: the art of managing IT based on a solid framework leveraging the company's political ecosystem. Springer, Berlin

Part V

Control

Measuring the Success of Data Governance

7

Abstract

Professionally managed data is the basis for goal-oriented corporate development in the context of digital transformation and thus also the basis for data-driven process optimization and the resulting competitive advantages. This is why it is so important for companies to address the professional management of data in an ever-changing and increasingly complex digital world and to recognize the value of Data Governance for the organization.

A final building block for the development of successful Data Governance is an accompanying measurement of success. In this chapter, we will discuss how the capabilities, services, and maturity levels of a company's own Data Management can be measured, evaluated, and compared with set development goals. To do so, the use of a capability maturity model (CMM), which measures the ranks of Data Management services along the company's processes (e.g., on a five-level maturity scale from "Aware" to "Optimizing"), is an established method.

7.1 Data Governance Maturity Model

It has proven to be good practice to start a performance measurement with a so-called zero measurement (De Haes 2016). This means that the state of the data organization is assessed comprehensively before the introduction of Data Governance, and thus before the first changes are introduced. This has several advantages. On the one hand, you get an unvarnished view of the initial situation and can adapt the upcoming measures even better to the further development of the ACTUAL state; on the other hand, you get a clear assessment of the ACTUAL situation, which ideally can also be used as part of the communication with internal stakeholders to show the urgency of the change and generate support.

© Springer-Verlag GmbH Germany, part of Springer Nature 2022
L. M. Bollweg, *Data Governance for Managers*, Management for Professionals,
https://doi.org/10.1007/978-3-662-65171-1_7

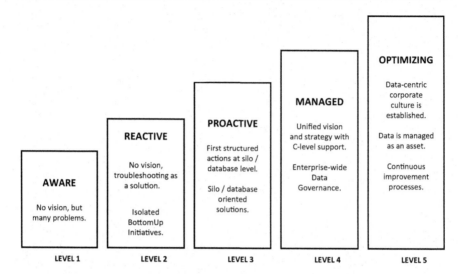

Fig. 7.1 Maturity model—Data Governance maturity model © Lars Michael Bollweg 2022. All Rights Reserved

---

Principle 30: A maturity assessment of the current state of development of the data organization is a useful starting point when implementing a Data Governance program.

Following the zero measurement, the performance measurement should be repeated at regular and predefined intervals, for example every six months. As a rule, the intervals should be long enough to allow the successes of the change to become visible and to be able to transparently present the progress within the organization.

When selecting a maturity model, one can either rely on established solutions such as the Data Governance maturity models from Gartner or IBM, or use one of the many related interpretations (Ladley 2012; Templar 2017; Seiner 2014). The maturity model presented in this book is based on these same established Data Governance capability maturity models from Gartner and IBM (De Haes 2016), but is varied in several components and simplified in measurement. The respective assessment of the maturity level of a company is made along a five-level scale of maturity levels (see Fig. 7.1).

Level 1 (Aware) This level represents the lowest maturity level of Data Governance. "Aware" describes companies in which no vision for Data Governance has yet been formulated and no description has been provided of how Data Governance would impact on corporate objectives. At this level, acceptance of standards, uniform processes, and models is low. While individual organizational units understand the importance of data in the enterprise and are trying to develop solutions using enterprise data, they are not finding the necessary support to overcome many data problems. There are simply no data initiatives in these companies that offer structured approaches to solving data problems.

Level 2 (Reactive) Companies at this "Reactive" level are generally aware of the importance of data for the success of the company. Whenever data problems are identified, IT and data projects are initiated to solve the data problems that arise in isolated measures (troubleshooting). Initial structuring measures or norms and standards emerge from Data Management to deal with the data quality problems that arise. However, it is difficult to enforce compliance with the standards and processes developed, because the organizational change required for this is not lived across all hierarchical levels.

Level 3 (Proactive) The "Proactive" level describes companies that are in the final phase of establishing professional Data Management. These companies are characterized in particular by an intensive and structured examination of their data inventory and the associated data flows, e.g., through data quality monitoring. They address data problems proactively, i.e., they try to identify impending business problems caused by poor data quality at an early stage and solve the causal data problems before the problem occurs. At this level, companies have already recognized that professional Data Management and Data Governance are necessary and a basic requirement for the successful handling of data in companies. At this level, operational responsibility is already firmly regulated and the relevant norms and standards are adhered to, but Data Management does not yet follow a uniform strategy that is known and accepted across the hierarchy, and professional Data Management is not yet part of the corporate culture and is therefore not yet practiced independently within the departments.

Level 4 (Managed) At this level, data and information are a valuable asset for the company. The norms and standards around information management are fully implemented and understood. The entire organization (Data Management and specialist department) uses these in projects within the company. In addition, professional Data Management has been set up and takes over the maintenance of the data inventory together with the specialist departments. The data organization consists of defined data spaces, which are supported by different roles to solve data problems across departments and functions. At this level, companies have, on the one hand, developed metrics to measure the progress and, more importantly, the success of Data Governance in the company. On the other hand, data is classified to enable efficient use of data, but also to ensure effective information security and data protection measures. Data Management at these companies follows a uniform strategy that is known and accepted across the hierarchy. The professional handling of data is part of the corporate culture and is practiced independently within Data Management and the specialist departments.

Level 5 (Optimizing) At the highest level, Data Governance is a fixed and significant component of the company organization. The established professional Data Management consistently identifies data-driven improvement potentials and permanently develops the business processes (increases productivity and efficiency) and the system landscape (identifies automation and workflow potentials) from the data perspective. In companies at the "Optimizing" maturity level, Data Governance is more than a problem-solving unit; it is a driver of digital transformation and optimizes and shapes future corporate development along data-centric value streams.

In order to assess the current maturity level, companies need to classify themselves at the individual levels of the Data Governance Maturity Model. The questionnaire in the following chapter can be used as support and as a simple aid for orientation.

7.2   Self-Assessment of the Current Development Status of the Data Governance Implementation

To measure the success of a Data Governance implementation, a self-assessment is needed in advance as a zero measurement. Where are the company and the data organization at the current time? For this purpose, various criteria must be used for evaluation, such as the status of the vision, is there a data strategy, and to what extent are the operational processes of Data Governance already developed.

It is normal for companies to be at different levels in the development status of individual criteria. This means that while there may already be an existing and accepted data strategy in the company, the implementation of the operational processes has not yet reached the breadth within the organization. Each company must be considered individually here and picked up where it is at the moment. This means that different measures must be taken for each company in order to establish professional Data Management. Nevertheless, self-assessment helps as a compass to identify these measures. With the help of the following questionnaire, a company can roughly assess the level at which the company's Data Management and data organization is.

For self-assessment, orientation along the broad lines of Data Management is recommended. Do not try to rank your organization better than it is, but remain self-critical. If you have not yet reached the maturity levels expected by you in this assessment, do not see it as a flaw; see it as an incentive to reach the next possible development level.

Aware
If you can answer "Yes" to any of the following questions, your company has reached the "Aware" maturity level:

1. Is the company aware that many problems and much untapped potential are due to poor Data Management?

2. Does your company already have initial initiatives or projects to develop a structured approach to solving data problems?
3. Is a Data Management department in formation or a Data Governance program in the planning stages?

Reactive
If you can answer "Yes" to **any** of the following questions, your company has reached the "Reactive" maturity level:

1. Does your company have employees from specialist departments (not Data Management) who respond to and rectify any data problems that arise?
2. Does your organization have a Data Management department that responds to data issues as they arise and remediates those issues?

Proactive
If you can answer "Yes" to **any** of the following questions, your company has reached the "Proactive" maturity level:

1. Does your company have a Data Management department that monitors the quality of the company's data and proactively points out potential problems and resolves them before they occur?
2. When solving data problems, does your company analyze the surrounding systems and data processes (CRUD and ETL) in a structured manner and ensure the sustainability of the solution found by taking these into account?

Managed
If you can answer "Yes" to **all** of the following questions, your company has reached the "Managed" maturity level:

1. Does your company have a data strategy?
2. Is your company's data strategy approved by management and is implementation ensured within a Data Governance framework?
3. Are data owners named in your company and are data spaces and data domains clearly assigned to them?

Optimizing
If you can answer "Yes" to **the** following question, your company has reached the "Optimizing" maturity level:

1. Does your company optimize the further development of corporate processes and business models along data-centric value streams and use the resulting knowledge as a driver for the digital transformation of the company?

Bibliography

De Haes S (2016) Enterprise governance of information technology: achieving alignment and value, featuring COBIT 5. Springer, Berlin

Ladley J (2012) Data governance: how to design, deploy and sustain an effective data governance program. Academic Press, Cambridge

Seiner R (2014) Non-invasive data governance: the path of least resistance and greatest success. Technics Publications, New Jersey

Templar M (2017) Get governed: building world class data governance programs. Ivory Lady Publishing, Wexford

List of Principles

8

Abstract

As in any technical book, you will find a great deal of information and practical instructions for action in this one, which unfortunately are all too often quickly forgotten after reading the book. To counteract this phenomenon at least somewhat, all the important principles for the implementation and successful operation of Data Governance have once again been highlighted separately and included in the following list. Use this list of principles as a shortcut to remember the most important contents of the book and to reflect on the procedure suggested in this book and to compare it with your own planning.

Principles "Basics"

Principle 1: Data Governance anchors Data Management in the organizational and operational structure of a company. Data Governance ensures that data responsibilities, coordination and optimization processes, as well as procedural models and standards are practiced uniformly and transparently throughout the company.

Principle 2: Data Governance creates complexity reduction to help the business manage data challenges.

Principle 3: Data Governance stands for holistic management of data along the entire data lifecycle.

Principle 4: Data responsibility is the organizational solution to the complex coordination challenges that arise from the high interconnectedness of data flows within an organization.

Principle 5: Data responsibility is assigned according to the creator principle.

Principle 6: Data responsibility lies with top management.

Principle 7: Data Governance is a role-based form of organization.

Principle 8: Role inclusion is one of the fundamentals of organizational planning for Data Governance and states that management should identify employees to

L. M. Bollweg, *Data Governance for Managers*, Management for Professionals,
https://doi.org/10.1007/978-3-662-65171-1_8

participate in Data Governance who have also managed the data prior to the implementation of Data Governance.

Principle 9: The roles of Data Governance should be filled equally by the business units and the IT-related departments. Data Governance is a driver for business and IT integration.

Principle 10: Data sets are structured and comprised in corporate data spaces.

Principle 11: Data owners set strategic goals and delegate operational implementation to data stewards.

Principle 12: Data Governance is most effective as an integrative part of the operational process and business unit organization.

Principle 13: Data Governance develops a lean, structured organization consisting of data owners and corporate data spaces.

Principle 14: Data Governance enables process-oriented management of data challenges.

Principles "Design"

Principle 15: For successful implementation of Data Governance, management must recognize the value of data and allocate the necessary resources for its implementation.

Principle 16: Before implementing Data Governance, at least one clear implementation driver must be identified. This should show the company in which areas Data Governance solves important business problems and thus generate a willingness to change.

Principle 17: Data Management skills are more than just data skills. A proactive mindset and a common language are equally critical to success.

Principle 18: Data quality can only be measured if the data requirements have been captured beforehand and validated against the data. Knowledge about data requirements is just as valuable to a company as knowledge about the data itself.

Principle 19: The successful implementation of Data Governance is based on a suitable organizational model and a suitable scaling model.

Principle 20: To sustain top-level support, Data Governance must generate measurable added value for the company from the outset and communicate this.

Principle 21: Data Governance promotes a data-centric corporate culture and benefits from it at the same time. Data Governance is therefore also always change management and development of the corporate culture.

Principles "Implement"

Principle 22: The Data Governance Operating Model is both a detailed visual and a detailed process description of the procedures of the Data Governance enterprise functions.

Principle 23: Data Governance is most effectively implemented within a matrix organization. But classic line organizations also benefit from professional Data Management.

Principle 24: Implement Data Governance in five stages: (1) on-boarding, (2) establishing data transparency, (3) tailoring data spaces and staff roles, (4) empowering data spaces, and (5) initiating regular operation.

Principle 25: The regular operation of Data Governance is a cycle of (1) understanding data, (2) identifying pain points and areas for improvement, (3) implementing data projects, and (4) monitoring data development.

Principles "Run"

Principle 26: Digital transformation is the continuous optimization and further development of digital tools in the company.

Principle 27: The five digital value creation stages serve as a compass and support for the target planning of data-driven development projects.

Principle 28: Data Governance as a Data Management tool is a fundamental component of the business architecture. But Data Governance is only one important component of three. Data Governance complements process and IT system management in the business architecture to provide a unified view of data, processes, and IT systems.

Principle 29: Data-driven value stream optimization helps companies identify digital development potential.

Principle 30: A maturity assessment of the current state of development of the data organization is a useful starting point when implementing a Data Governance program.

Bonus: Data Definition Template

9

Abstract

In addition to successfully setting up a data organization, knowledge about data and how to handle this knowledge is a key competence for successfully meeting the challenges of digital transformation in companies. Understanding the significance of data in systems and databases is the basis for broad data knowledge in the company and the foundation for good Data Governance. Many companies today still do not follow a uniform and structured standard for the definition of data and therefore have to invest unnecessarily high efforts to establish a common knowledge base within teams and projects.

In the following, therefore, a template is presented for the uniform and structured definition of data, which should sensibly be used within a modern data catalog. Of course, the use of a software solution is the most convenient but also the most expensive solution. However, a structured data definition can also be collected and provided to the company within Excel and other data processing programs. Knowing and understanding one's own data inventory is not a question of budget, but a question of professional Data Management.

What is a structured data definition? A structured data definition clearly and understandably explains the meaning and context of a data element, a data object, or a data table.

What are the goals of a structured data definition? The following specifications for data definitions aim to reduce ambiguities in the course of writing data definitions and to improve the readability and general comprehensibility of data definitions.

Which standards does the data definition follow? The data definition proposed here has been developed according to ISO/IEC 11179 (Metadata Registry (MDR) standard) and structured according to Stanford University data definition standards.

© Springer-Verlag GmbH Germany, part of Springer Nature 2022   155
L. M. Bollweg, *Data Governance for Managers*, Management for Professionals,
https://doi.org/10.1007/978-3-662-65171-1_9

Table 9.1 Quality criteria for data definitions

Concise	As short as possible, as long as necessary
Precise	Clear and unambiguous in its message
Simple	Understandable, written in non-technical language
Unmistakable	The description of a data element must be clearly different from the description of other data elements
Non self-referring	The name of the data element to be described must not be used to describe the data element itself
Single	The understanding of the definition of a data element must not depend on other data definitions or other external information. The data definition must not contain any content other than the data definition itself

Table 9.2 Structuring principles

General classification (The data element is a...)	The class or type of term to be defined
Properties/delimiters (The data element has/describes...)	Properties that distinguish the term being described from other definitions
Function and requirement description (Is used/required for...)	A description of what the data element being described is used or needed for

Table 9.3 Optional extensions

Related terms	If synonyms or similar terms are used for the same data element in the company, these terms must be documented in the data definition
Abbreviations	If abbreviations are used in the company for a data element, these abbreviations should be documented in the data definition
Deepening/ Context	Descriptions or explanations necessary for understanding, e.g., scales of categorical values and/or speaking keys (reference data)
Notes/Links	If useful references as well as links to maintenance instructions are helpful, they can be entered here. Example: If a term is no longer used in the company and has been replaced by another term, the reference to the new term should also be documented as a link in the data definition, if necessary

What are quality criteria for a good data definition? A well-written data definition is (see Table 9.1):

Which components does a structured data definition consist of? Whenever possible, the structure of a data definition should consist of the following building blocks (see Tables 9.2 and 9.3):

Basics

Optional Extension

How do you ensure a uniform notation? All data definitions should always begin in the same way and be written in complete sentences (see Table 9.4):

Table 9.4 Standardization of data definitions

Data elements	Data objects	Data tables
"The data element of column 'X' is a... " If the data element is an attribute of an object, the object must be named first: "The data element of column 'X' is an attribute of data object 'X.'"	"The data object 'X' is a..."	"The data table 'X' is a..."

Fig. 9.1 Data definition blocks © Lars Michael Bollweg 2022. All Rights Reserved

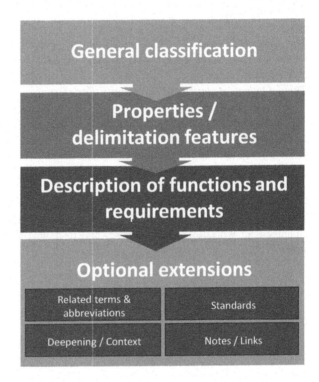

What does an example of a complete data definition look like? In the following, the structure and then a complete data definition is shown by means of an example (see Fig. 9.1).

Example Data Definition for the Column "Customer Number":

1. **General classification**

   The data element of the "Customer number" column is part of the "Customer master data" data object and contains the unique identification number of a customer.

2. **Properties/delimitation features**

   The data element consists of eight digits. For existing customers, the eight digits are preceded by "CU."

3. **Description of functions and requirements**

The data element is used in all commercial systems for unique identification of customers.

4. **Optional additions**

   Related terms and abbreviations: CU = Customer
   Standards: International customer number key

Of course, the headings used here are not needed, so a final data definition follows the pattern below:

The data element of the "Customer number" column is part of the "Customer master data" data object and contains the unique identification number of a customer.

The data element consists of eight digits. For existing customers, the eight digits are preceded by "CU."

The data element is used in all commercial systems for unique identification of customers.

Related terms and abbreviations: CU = Customer

Standards: International customer number key

Data definitions are a valuable tool for managing data. By adding the roles assigned in Data Governance, they also have the potential to accelerate Data Management workflows and processes and to reduce research efforts and waiting times.

Closing Words

10

Abstract

Congratulations, you made it to the end of this book. Data Governance is an abstract topic for which there is "unfortunately" "no one-fits-all solution." Every Data Governance implementation is different because every company is different, too. But you could see, there is a wealth of experience to build on and a variety of basic principles to guide you in implementing and operating Data Governance. Now your work begins.

However, we hope that we have been able to give you a good introduction and a clear idea of the topic of Data Governance with this book and have thus prepared you well for the upcoming challenges in the course of your Data Governance implementation. Our goal was and is to provide you with a template for Data Governance implementation that you can use as inspiration for developing your own Data Governance program. It is our concern that more companies realize the benefits of professional Data Management and start to use them for their own benefit with the help of Data Governance.

That is why we will continue to work in the future to ensure that data responsibility is assigned in every company, that the data space logic is established and lived, and that data quality is monitored and improved. Because the key to the targeted further development of companies in the digital age—the digital transformation—only lies in the synchronization of data, processes, and systems. What is meant is the digital transformation of these companies, but also the digital transformation of our economy and society as a whole. Unfortunately, it is already high time for this; digitalization will not wait. Let's get to work on it.

At the beginning of this book, we promised you that you would learn about a variety of content, process models, and methods. Now we offer you the opportunity to take our word for it. By now you should know and understand the following topics. If this is not the case, please check again at the indicated places in the book:

© Springer-Verlag GmbH Germany, part of Springer Nature 2022   159
L. M. Bollweg, *Data Governance for Managers*, Management for Professionals,
https://doi.org/10.1007/978-3-662-65171-1_10

The answer to the question of what is Data Governance and professional Data Management can be found in detail in Chap. 3 and again in more depth in Chaps. 4, 5, and 6.

The answer to the question of what capabilities your Data Management team needs to operate successful Data Governance can be found in Chap. 4.

The answer to the question of how to develop an implementation strategy for Data Governance can be found in Chaps. 4 and 5.

The answer to the question of what roles exist in Data Governance can be found in Chap. 4.

The answer to the question of how to assign data responsibility can be found in Chaps. 2, 4, and 5.

The answer to the question of how you can use data projects to directly generate added value for the company and thus a high level of acceptance for the implementation of Data Governance can be found in Chaps. 4, 6, and 7.

The answer to the question of how to optimize, harmonize, and End2End manage data, processes, and systems via the value contributions of Data Governance, and which methods help you do this, can be found in Chaps. 6 and 7.

The answer to the question of how you can implement and establish a data-centric corporate culture via Data Governance and use it as a driver of digital transformation can be found by bringing together all the chapters in this book when developing your own Data Governance.

With all this information, we can now only wish you success in your daily work in Data Management and in implementing your Data Governance. Use these many insights, process models, and methods from this book to develop your department, your company. Be the driver of digital transformation. Let's go.

Glossary

Artificial Intelligence Artificial Intelligence (AI) is an umbrella term for machines learning human-like intelligence using various learning methods.

Business Architecture Business architecture uses various methods, e.g., from enterprise architecture, to further develop value-creating processes, data and IT systems and to represent them in artifacts.

Change Management Process A change management process (change process) is understood as a temporary change from an ACTUAL state to a TARGET state.

Control Date The regular meeting (Jour Fixe) is a regularly scheduled appointment that arranges the meeting of a small group of people.

Core Process A core process comprises all activities that contribute to the value creation of a company.

Corporate Culture Corporate culture refers to the values, norms, and symbols of organizational members that contribute to the long-term success of the company.

Data Data is descriptions of reality, i.e., facts, measurements, or observations from the real world.

Data and Information Flows The terms generally refer to the data trace within the system landscape in the company. In other words, the flow of data and information from a data source to a data sink.

Data-driven Corporate Culture A data-driven corporate culture is characterized by decisions being made on the basis of data and information. Data is recognized as an important and valuable asset for companies and is managed professionally accordingly.

Data Governance The term Data Governance stands for the holistic management of data in a company.

Data Governance Maturity Model The Data Governance Maturity Model is used to evaluate and rank an organization in Maturity Levels.

Data Literacy Data literacy or data competence describes the professional handling of data. It is an ability to interpret, analyze, and visualize data.

Data Management Data Management is the professional management of data along the data lifecycle. Data should be managed in a requirements-oriented manner.

Data Projects Data projects are used to further develop data and digital infrastructures in order to generate added value for the company.

© Springer-Verlag GmbH Germany, part of Springer Nature 2022   161
L. M. Bollweg, *Data Governance for Managers*, Management for Professionals,
https://doi.org/10.1007/978-3-662-65171-1

Data Protection Data protection is intended to prevent unauthorized access to data, in particular personal data, and thus protect the right to informational self-determination.

Data Quality High data quality is understood as the fulfillment and thus successful validation of business requirements against the data.

Data Quality Management Data quality management ensures and improves data quality in the company in the long term.

Data Responsibility The goal of Data Governance is to ensure that each data set is assigned to a responsible person within the company. There are different approaches to assigning data responsibility (e.g., political, thematic, structural).

Data Security Data security prevents the loss and manipulation of data through technical and organizational measures.

Database Databases store and manage a large amount of data.

Database System A database system consists of the database management system, which manages databases, and the data to be managed, i.e., the database.

Decision Support Decision Support is designed to provide key information to decision-makers (e.g., via reporting and dashboards).

Digital Transformation Digital transformation is an ongoing change process characterized by the introduction and use of digital tools and applications.

E2E The abbreviation stands for End2End and represents a temporally and factually closed process (from beginning to end) that serves to fulfill a (customer) requirement.

Enterprise Architecture The enterprise architecture provides an overview of the interaction between IT and the business of a company and thus achieves efficiency increases.

ETL ETL stands for Extract, Transform and Load. ETL is a data integration process that extracts relevant data from various sources (E), then transforms the data into the schema and format of a target database (T), and finally loads the data into the database (L).

GDPR The EU GDPR is a European General Data Protection Regulation that sets out rules for the processing of personal data.

Information When data is assigned a context or meaning, it becomes information.

Innovation Project An innovation project serves to develop new solutions, business ideas or products. Frequently, iterative and agile process models are used as part of the development and implementation.

Interoperability Interoperability is used for smooth communication and cooperation between different IT systems in a company.

JSON JSON (JavaScript Object Notation) is a data format in a readable text form for exchanging data between IT systems.

Maturity Level The maturity level is used to evaluate Data Governance in a company. Various criteria are used for this purpose.

NoSQL NoSQL are databases that do not follow a relational approach. NoSQL databases are often suitable for storing large amounts of data.

Operating Model The operating model is used to define and document a standard operating procedure and to further develop Data Governance.

Operational Excellence Operational excellence defines that the value-adding processes of a company are continuously optimized and implemented.

Organizational Structure The organizational plan provides an overview of the entire line organization of a company.

Predictive Analytics Predictive analytics is a method of analysis that uses historical data to predict future events.

Process Management Process management is often a department that applies various methods to control and optimize business processes in a company.

Process Organization The process organization describes work processes from a time and location perspective that pursue a specific objective in the company.

Project Management Project management refers to various methods that include activities for the successful implementation of a project.

Reporting Reporting contains information about the company in the form of tables, documents, or figures.

Responsive Organization Responsive organization is an umbrella term for keeping organizations organizationally responsive and adaptable in an ever-changing and increasingly complex environment.

SQL SQL (Structured Query Language) is a database language that includes activities for creating and managing a database.

Stakeholders Stakeholders are different interest groups that have diverse requirements for the company.

Steering Committee The steering committee is a body in a project that consists of people who have a high interest in the success of the project. The committee is supposed to answer important questions to the project management and steer the project.

System Architecture The system architecture shows a detailed overview of all IT systems in the company, including interfaces to other IT systems.

Use Case A use case describes a function in an IT system based on a model.

Validation Rules Validation rules increase the data quality in an IT system. Validation rules check user input against defined rules.

Value Stream Analysis Value Stream Analysis separates the value-creating activities of a company from those that need to be improved and thus do not add value.

Value Stream Mapping Value Stream Mapping is used to visualize the most important and thus value-adding activities and their data.

XML XML (Extensible Markup Language) is a markup language for representing data hierarchically in a structured form.

Printed by Printforce, United Kingdom